JAMES MCNAIR's
PASTA
COOKBOOK

Photography by Patricia Brabant

Chronicle Books • San Francisco

Printed in Japan

Library of Congress
Cataloging-in-Publication Data
McNair, James K.
James McNair's Pasta Cookbook/
photography by Patricia Brabant.
p. cm.
Includes index.
ISBN 0-87701-648-8.
ISBN 0-87701-618-6 (pbk.)
1. Cookery (Pasta)
I. Brabant, Patricia.
II. Title.
TX809.M17M393 1990
641.8'22—dc20   90-44806
                                    CIP

Distributed in Canada by
Raincoast Books
112 East Third Avenue
Vancouver, British Columbia V5T 1C8

10 9 8 7 6 5 4 3 2 1

Chronicle Books
275 Fifth Street
San Francisco, California 94103

Cold Pasta, the first book in this single-subject series, was dedicated to Lin Cotton, the finest friend and partner anyone could ever imagine. As hot pasta is probably his favorite food, this volume is for Lin, again, with all the same gratitude and love that was expressed some seventeen books ago. Without his assistance and encouragement this book series simply would not have happened.

Produced by The Rockpile Press, San Francisco and Lake Tahoe

Text, recipes, photographic and food styling, and book design by James McNair

Editorial production assistance by Lin Cotton

Editorial and styling assistance by Ellen Berger-Quan

Photography by Patricia Brabant

Photographic Art Direction by James McNair and Patricia Brabant

Photographic assistance by M. J. Murphy

Typography and mechanical production by Cleve Gallat and David Kingins of CTA Graphics

CONTENTS

A NEW WORLD
OF PASTA
AND NOODLES

It is sometimes difficult to remember only a few years back when pasta as a word and a food was virtually unknown throughout much of America. Oh, yes, we had our macaroni and cheese and what we thought to be Italian fare—mushy spaghetti and meatballs, overcooked lasagna, and ravioli smothered in tin-tasting tomato sauce. In Chinese cafes we ate wonton or chow mein, and sometimes slurped noodles from broth in Japanese restaurants. During the past several years of rapidly expanding food knowledge and under the influence of a new breed of creative chefs and food writers, pasta and noodles from the far corners of the world have taken their rightful place as premier foods from coast to coast.

Although the noodle was probably a staple in China some 1,500 years before it made its way to Italy, for many of us pasta is closely identified with Italian cooking, possibly because no one prepares it better. But this marvelous food no longer belongs to Italy or China alone. As with all our culinary imports, we've learned to be creative, not bound by traditions. Pasta is now made in every shade of the rainbow and in shapes and sizes that would cause heart failure among Italian purists. We toss and sauce pasta with indigenous ingredients from the Southwest and Louisiana Cajun country, and with the celebrated bounties of California. East has joined West as we adorn Asian noodles with European sauces and crown Italian pasta with ingredients from the Orient.

On the next several pages you will find rather detailed directions for making, shaping, and cooking your own fresh Italian-style pasta or Asian-style noodles. When homemade pasta is adeptly made, nothing beats its delicate texture. Unless you practice the art of pasta making frequently enough to master the technique, however, it is probably best to cook dried pasta, although that may seem like heresy to pasta purists. Dried pasta certainly cooks up far better than any of the "fresh" pastas I've tried from supermarket refrigerator cases. As with any ingredient, the quality of dried pasta varies greatly. Choose a brand made of hard durum wheat, which will render cooked pasta that is al dente, or tender but still firm to the bite.

Some of us are lucky enough to have fresh pasta shops nearby that prepare fairly decent versions of Italian-style pasta. I frequently purchase whole large sheets that are the perfect size to serve as a layer in lasagna, or I cut the sheets into any shape desired.

In San Francisco, as in other major cities, we are also fortunate to have numerous markets that carry a wide variety of fresh Asian noodles. When I'm at my Lake Tahoe retreat, however, I must make my own Asian-style noodles or, more frequently, rely on dried ones.

I've divided the pasta recipes in this book into two sections. EAST contains recipes using Asian noodles, such as Chinese *mein,* Japanese *udon* or *soba,* and Southeast Asian rice noodles. Most of the recipes are authentic versions of the varied Asian cuisines; others are my westernized interpretation.

In the WEST section you will find recipes for European and American pasta classics along with representatives of the new age of cooking that blend techniques and ingredients from all over the world.

Throughout this book I've used a number of unusual-looking pastas that are either delicately or strongly flavored with vegetable or fruit purées, herbs, spices, coffee, or other additions to enliven your palate. For the sake of dramatic presentation or just plain fun, I've also introduced some new colors to the pasta palette. Keep in mind, however, that almost every recipe in this book can be made with either homemade or store-bought fresh pasta or with a wide range of dried macaroni and noodle products that make pasta cookery quick and easy.

At the back of the book are a few of my favorite basic sauce recipes. Although some of these are components of more complex dishes, any of them can stand alone as a pasta topping.

Basic Pasta

About 2 cups all-purpose flour,
preferably unbleached
3 large eggs, at room temperature
1 teaspoon olive oil, preferably
extra-virgin (optional)
½ teaspoon salt (optional)

All-purpose flour yields the most tender pasta. If you wish a dough that remains firmer, substitute finely ground semolina, or hard-wheat durum flour, for all or part of the all-purpose flour. Other alternative flours that may be substituted for as much as half of the all-purpose flour include rice flour; finely ground yellow, white, blue, or red cornmeal; buckwheat flour; or whole-wheat flour.

Purist Italian pasta makers do not add oil, seasonings, or colorings to their pasta, other than the occasional spinach. We American cooks, however, aren't tradition bound and seem to be having more fun with pasta; our dough is often mildly flavored and colored with an array of natural foods. Following this basic recipe, you'll find numerous suggestions that offer variety to the wonderful old standard. The addition of a little oil makes the pasta easier to work with for the novice, and a bit of salt enhances the flavor. You'll note that directions for using electric machines that extrude pasta are missing, since I find the results to be unsatisfactory. If you choose to use these machines, follow the manufacturer's instructions.

To make pasta dough by hand, shape 2 cups flour into a mound on a smooth work surface or in a large, shallow bowl. Place a fist in the center of the mound and move it in a circular motion to spread out the flour and form a wide, shallow well in the center.

Add the eggs, and oil and salt (if used), to the center of the well. Break the yolks lightly with a fork. With a circular motion of the fork or with your fingertips, draw flour from the inside wall of the well and gradually incorporate it into the egg mixture. While mixing, use your free hand to maintain the wall of flour intact.

When the eggs are no longer runny, push most of the flour over them, reserving to one side any flour that you think will not be necessary. Knead the dough with both hands until it forms a crumbly mass. If the dough feels too sticky, gradually work in more flour. If it is too dry and crumbly, work in a few drops of water at a time.

Position the dough to one side of the work surface and scrape off all bits of flour and egg from the work surface with a flat metal dough scraper or a knife blade. Wash and dry your hands, then lightly sprinkle them and the work surface with the same type of flour used in the dough. Place the dough in the center of the flour-dusted area and knead by pressing down on it with the heels of your palms. Fold the dough in half over itself, give it a half turn, and repeat this kneading procedure until the dough feels very elastic and smooth and doesn't break apart when you pull it, 10 to 12 minutes. Knead in additional flour as necessary. Test the dough by inserting a finger into the center. If it comes out dry and clean, the dough has enough flour incorporated; if the finger is moist or has dough attached, more flour is required.

Shape the dough into a ball and dust it lightly with flour. Wrap in plastic wrap or cover with an inverted bowl and let stand at room temperature for at least 25 minutes or up to 2 hours to relax the dough.

To make pasta dough in a food processor, combine the ingredients in a processor and pulse until well mixed, then run the machine until the dough forms a ball. Transfer to a lightly floured surface and knead by hand as described in the preceding paragraphs. Form into a ball and let stand as described above.

After resting the dough, flatten, thin, shape, and stuff (if desired) as described on pages 14-21.

Makes about 1 pound, enough to serve 8 as a pasta course, or 4 as a main course.

PASTA EQUIPMENT

In addition to a large cooking pot and a colander for draining, here are a few items that aid the pasta cook.

PASTA ROLLING PIN. A perfectly straight extralong wooden pin without handles is best.

PASTRY WHEEL. Choose a plain or fluted blade for cutting noodles of any width as well as special shapes.

PASTA MACHINE. Although some people opt for electric-powered machines, the time-honored hand-cranked Atlas machine is inexpensive, reliable, and easy. Electric models that mix and extrude dough do not produce as tender a pasta as the hand-cranked machine or its electric-powered equivalent.

PASTA SERVER. A deep spoon with fat tines extended all around the bowl is indispensable for serving noodles.

CHEESE GRATER. For sprinkling cheese on top of pasta, I prefer the thin shreds achieved by a device with a hand-turned rolling grater drum placed inside a pair of handles held in the other hand; the cheese goes in a compartment formed where the handles join. When you wish pulverized hard cheese to stir into a sauce, the food processor yields a large quantity in a hurry.

Flavored Pasta Variations

HERB SPRIG PASTA

Arrange sprigs, leaflets, or individual leaves of fresh herbs on a sheet of thinly rolled fresh pasta. Brush a second sheet of pasta with water and lay it, moistened side down, over the herbs. Run the pasta through a pasta machine 2 or 3 times to adhere the two sheets. Using a knife, pastry roller, or cookie cutter, cut the pasta into squares, disks, leaves, or other shapes.

When preparing Basic Pasta, blend in any of the following. Additional flour may be necessary when kneading to accommodate the extra moisture in some ingredients. For pastas that will be served as sweets, add ½ cup powdered sugar along with the flour, if desired.

BLACK BEAN PASTA. Pour ½ cup liquid from cooked black beans into a small saucepan and boil until reduced by half. Add along with the eggs. Or add about 1 cup puréed cooked black beans along with the eggs.

CHILE PASTA. Add 3 tablespoons ground dried red hot chile such as *ancho,* cayenne, or *pasilla* along with the eggs. Or add ¼ cup puréed cooked fresh or dried chiles.

CHOCOLATE PASTA. Add ¼ cup powdered cocoa to the flour.

CITRUS PASTA. Add ¼ cup strained freshly squeezed juice and 2 to 3 tablespoons minced zest of lemon, lime, orange, tangerine, or other citrus along with the eggs.

COFFEE PASTA. Add ¼ cup espresso powder and ½ cup strongly brewed coffee along with the eggs.

CORN PASTA. Substitute ½ cup cornmeal for an equal amount of the flour. Add about ½ cup puréed fresh corn kernels along with the eggs.

FLAVORED-OIL PASTA. Add drops of extract oils such as peppermint, jasmine, rose, or citrus to taste along with the eggs. Look for edible flavored oils in drugstores, bath supply shops, natural foods stores, and gourmet shops. Pure extracts such as almond, peppermint, or vanilla may be substituted; add to taste.

FRUIT PASTA. Add ½ cup puréed fresh berries, banana, figs, mango, papaya, or other soft fruit, or ½ cup puréed cooked fresh apple or pear or dried fruit such as prune along with the eggs.

GARLIC PASTA. Sauté 3 tablespoons minced or pressed garlic in 1 tablespoon olive oil. Substitute this for the oil in the basic recipe.

GINGER PASTA. Add 3 tablespoons minced fresh ginger root along with the eggs.

GREEN TEA PASTA. Add about ½ cup strong freshly brewed green tea along with the eggs.

HERBED PASTA. Add ½ cup minced fresh herbs such as basil, cilantro (coriander), mint, tarragon, rosemary, marjoram, chives, or a favorite combination along with the eggs.

PEPPERCORN PASTA. Add 3 tablespoons crushed black, white, or Sichuan peppercorns along with the eggs.

SAFFRON PASTA. Dissolve ½ teaspoon crumbled saffron threads in 2 tablespoons warm water. Add along with the eggs.

SEEDED PASTA. Add 3 tablespoons lightly toasted caraway, poppy, or sesame seeds along with the eggs.

SPICED PASTA. Add 1 to 3 tablespoons, or according to taste, ground spice such as cardamom, cinnamon, cumin, curry powder, nutmeg, or vanilla bean along with the eggs.

SQUID-INK PASTA. Collect black liquid from the ink sac of large cuttlefish. Or purchase frozen packets of squid ink from importers of fancy foods. Add about 2 tablespoons along with the eggs.

TOMATO PASTA. Add 3 tablespoons tomato paste along with the eggs.

VEGETABLE PASTA. Cook about ½ pound fresh beets, broccoli, carrots, green peas, spinach, sweet peppers, or other vegetable or about 8 ounces frozen vegetable until tender. Drain the vegetables and squeeze to release as much moisture as possible. Purée in a food processor or blender. Add along with the eggs.

NEW COLORED PASTA

For festive presentations or just plain fun, try these ideas that will probably send pasta purists into cardiac arrest. Food color pastes are available from stores that sell cake decorating supplies.

MARBLEIZED PASTA. Near the end of kneading fresh pasta, add food color paste; do not overblend. Choose colors that are compatible with any flavors added to the pasta; try bright pink food color and peppermint oil or add streaks of orange food color to yellow saffron pasta.

NEON PASTA. Add generous amounts of food color paste along with the eggs when making fresh pasta. To vividly color dried pasta products, add a generous amount of food color paste to the boiling water before adding pasta.

PASTEL PASTA. Add food color paste or liquid when making fresh pasta dough; use appropriate colors to intensify vegetable purée additions. Or subtly color the water as described above.

Asian Wheat Noodles

2 eggs
¼ cup cold water
About 2 cups all-purpose flour
Additional flour for dusting

In a bowl, combine the eggs and water and beat to mix. Stir in about 1½ cups of the flour and quickly mix with a wooden spoon until the dough begins to stick together. Turn out onto a flour-dusted work surface.

Knead the dough until smooth and no longer sticky, adding flour, a little at a time, if necessary. Cover with a dish towel or inverted bowl and let stand about 30 minutes to relax dough.

Roll dough, cut by hand or in a hand-cranked pasta machine, and stuff (if desired) as described on pages 14-21.

Cook as described on pages 22-23; for authentic Asian-style noodles, cook until a bit softer than the still-firm-to-the-bite stage favored for most pasta.

Makes about 1 pound, enough to serve 8 as a pasta course, or 4 as a main course.

Asian Rice Noodles

The flour and two starch powders may be purchased in Asian markets and some natural foods stores.

In a bowl, combine the flour, starches, salt, and water and beat with a wooden spoon until smooth. Strain the mixture through a fine wire sieve into a clean bowl. Add the oil and mix well. Set aside for about 30 minutes.

Position a steamer rack over boiling water and grease two or more shallow 8- or 9-inch square pans with oil. Fill a larger pan with about ½ inch cold water. Set aside.

Stir the noodle batter to recombine. Pour enough of the batter into one of the greased pans to evenly coat the bottom, about ½ cup. Place the pan on the steamer rack, cover with a cloth towel to prevent excess condensation from dropping on the noodles, cover the steamer, and steam for 5 minutes. Transfer the noodle pan to the container of cold water and let stand until cool. Cook the remaining batter in the same way.

When cooled, transfer the noodle sheet to a well-oiled baking sheet and lightly brush the top with oil. As the noodle sheets are oiled, stack them on a tray or plate. When all the dough is cooked, cover the stack tightly with plastic wrap and chill at least 2 hours or as long as overnight.

Use the chilled uncooked noodles as wrappers for stuffed pastas, or slice through the noodle sheets with a sharp knife to cut noodles of the desired width, then cook as described on pages 22-23.

Makes about 1 pound, enough to serve 8 as a first course, or 4 as a main course.

1¾ cups rice flour
½ cup tapioca starch
6 tablespoons wheat starch
2 teaspoons salt
3¼ cups water
3 tablespoons high-quality vegetable oil
Additional oil for coating

Flattening and Thinning

Rolling by hand.

Stretching while rolling.

To flatten and thin pasta dough by hand, lightly dust a clean, flat work surface with flour. If you wish, divide the dough into sections to make rolling easier; keep extra dough covered while working with one piece at a time. Position the dough in the center of the work surface and flatten it with your hands. Using a very long cylindrical rolling pin without handles, roll back and forth over the dough, without applying heavy downward pressure, until dough is about ⅛ inch thick. After each roll turn the dough a quarter turn to keep it from sticking to the surface. When the dough has been flattened to the correct thickness, begin to curl the dough around the rolling pin. As you pull the dough back and forth with the pin, move your cupped hands along the length of the pin to further stretch the dough in all directions. Work as quickly as possible to keep the dough from drying out, and continue to turn it each time you repeat the rolling and stretching. Dust with flour whenever the dough feels sticky. Roll and stretch until the dough is paper-thin, or a little thicker as directed in some recipes.

If the dough will be used for stuffed pasta, cut and fill immediately while pliable and still a bit sticky; it may crack or become too dry to adhere tightly if not used at once. If it will be cut into noodles, dust the dough with flour and let it dry for about 15 minutes for wide noodles or up to 25 minutes for thin noodles; turn the dough over several times during drying. It is ready for cutting when it no longer sticks to other pieces of dough but is still pliable and soft.

Smoothing by machine.　　　　*Thinning the dough.*

To flatten and thin pasta dough with a hand-cranked pasta machine,
set the machine on its widest opening. Pull off a piece of the dough about
the size of an egg; keep the remaining dough covered to prevent it from
drying out. Feed the piece of dough through the pasta machine until it is
very smooth and elastic, 8 to 10 times. Each time the dough strip comes
out, fold it in half before feeding it into the machine again. If the dough
becomes sticky, dust lightly with flour. Adjust the roller to the next setting
and pass the dough through, this time leaving the strip unfolded. Roll the
dough through the machine 1 or 2 more times at the same opening.
Continue feeding the strip of dough through the rollers, narrowing the
opening down one step every 2 or 3 times to thin out the dough to the
desired degree. Avoid rolling too thin or the dough may crack and
disintegrate during cooking. Repeat the rolling and thinning with the
remaining dough.

Cut dough for stuffed pasta immediately; if cutting noodles, let the dough
rest as previously described.

Cutting with a wheel and ruler.

Shaping with a cookie cutter.

Using a pattern.

Cutting and Shaping

Whether the dough has been thinned by hand or in a hand-cranked machine, strips for lasagna, extrawide ribbons, any stuffed pasta, or fanciful shapes must be cut by hand. To cut straight edges, use a metal ruler as a guide and cut with a sharp knife or a plain or fluted rolling pastry wheel. To cut discs, use saucers, drinking glasses, or biscuit or cookie cutters. For fanciful or geometric shapes, use cookie cutters, or draw and cut out a paper template, lay it over the pasta, and cut with a sharp knife.

To cut noodles by hand, position a metal ruler on the flat sheet of dough and cut the dough into the desired width with a sharp knife or a plain or fluted rolling pastry wheel; cut to about ⅙ inch wide for tagliarini, ⅛ inch

Rolling and cutting with a knife.

Cutting noodles by machine.

Forming multicolored pasta.

wide for fettuccine, ¼ inch wide for *tagliatelle,* 1 inch or wider for *pappardelle.* Separate the noodles and spread them out to dry, preferably on cloth towels, for about 15 minutes. Alternatively, roll up the dough sheet jelly-roll fashion, then flatten the top slightly and cut with a sharp knife across the roll into desired widths. Unroll and let dry as above.

To cut noodles with a hand-cranked pasta machine, adjust the blades of the machine to the selected cutting width, then roll each dried strip of pasta through the machine. Hang or spread the noodles out to dry again for about 15 minutes.

MULTICOLORED PASTA SHEETS

Prepare fresh pasta in two or more colors and flavors. Using a hand-cranked pasta machine, roll out each pasta into wide strips as described on page 15. Cover the strips of one color and set aside while you cut the other pieces of pasta into noodles. Do not allow to dry.

Lightly brush a strip of the wide pasta with water, then overlay it with the colored noodles to form a desired pattern, leaving some space between the noodles for the wide strip to show through. Press the colored pasta with your fingertips to seal. Dust the pasta with flour and run it through the pasta machine a couple of times to bind the colors together.

Alternatively, cut all the pasta into noodles, then moisten the edges and arrange the noodles in alternating colors. Press with your fingertips to seal. Dust the pasta lightly with flour and run it through a hand-cranked pasta machine to bind the colors together.

Forming cappelletti.

Stuffing

Prepare fresh pasta and roll it out to about ¹⁄₁₆ inch, or purchase takeout fresh pasta sheets. Work on a flour-dusted surface and keep any extra pasta covered to keep it from drying out.

Some cooks substitute Chinese square wonton wrappers or rectangular egg-roll wrappers or Japanese round *gyōza* skins for fresh pasta when making cappelletti, ravioli, tortellini, or cannelloni. Fresh wrappers are available refrigerated in many supermarkets, or look for frozen ones and thaw before using. When using these wrappers for Italian-style filled pastas, let them come to room temperature, then roll them out a little thinner.

CANNELLONI. Cut pasta into rectangles 4 to 5 inches wide by 5 to 6 inches long. Add filling lengthwise in the center and roll up pasta jelly-roll fashion to form tubes.

CAPPELLETTI. Cut pasta into 2-inch squares. Add a dab of filling in the center and brush exposed dough with water or beaten egg. Diagonally fold the square so that the top corner does not quite meet the bottom corner and press to seal. Pick up the pasta, wrap it around a finger, and press the

Filling potstickers.   *Pleating potstickers.*

two outside opposite corners together; moisten corners with egg or water
if they won't adhere. The finished form should resemble a peaked bishop's
hat.

LASAGNA. Cut wide pasta strips into ribbons the length of the pan.
Without overlapping, position the pasta to completely cover bottom of pan
or a layer of filling; cut extra pasta to fill in any holes. Continue layering
pasta and filling.

POTSTICKERS OR *GYŌZA.* Use round wrappers made of fresh noodle
dough. Place about 2 teaspoons of filling just off center and use your
fingertips to shape it into a half circle. Moisten the inside edge of the dough
with beaten egg or water. Fold the wrapper over the filling so that the edges
meet, then pinch the center of the joined edges to adhere. On the side of
the dumpling facing you, and beginning just to one side of the pinched
center, fold the dough to form 3 little pleats, with edges facing toward the
center; pinch together at the top to seal tightly. Repeat the pleating on the
other side of the pinched center, reversing the folds so that the pleat edges
face the center. Leave the back side of the dumpling unpleated.

Stuffing cutout ravioli.

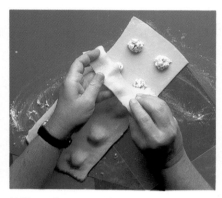

Filling sheet ravioli.

Cutting sheet ravioli.

RAVIOLI. Cut pasta into squares, circles, or other shapes of desired size. Mound filling in the center of half of the pieces and brush exposed dough with beaten egg. Cover with another piece of dough cut exactly the same, then press around the filling to eliminate air and seal the pasta. Sometimes, I allow a wide band of pasta to extend well beyond the filling; the extra pasta is delicious with the sauce, and the filling becomes a prized morsel.

Alternatively, spread out sheets of fresh pasta and drop mounds of filling on top, leaving about 2 inches of space between mounds. Brush exposed dough with beaten egg and cover each sheet with a second sheet of dough. Press sheets together firmly around the mounds of filling to eliminate air and seal dough. Cut between mounds of filling with a knife or pastry wheel to form squares, or cut out with a biscuit cutter to form circles. Or if you have a traditional ravioli mold, spread a sheet of pasta over the mold, spoon filling into cavities, cover with another sheet of pasta, and roll a ravioli cutter over top.

Filling spring rolls.

SPRING ROLLS. Use square or round wrappers made of fresh noodle dough, or extremely thin dried rice paper made from rice flour. Moisten wrappers (allow rice paper to soften), then place filling on lower third of each wrapper, leaving about 1 inch of space along the bottom and sides. Fold the bottom up around the filling, then tuck in each end to encase filling. Continue to roll to form a cylinder.

TORTELLINI. Cut pasta into 2-inch circles with a floured biscuit cutter or a glass. Spoon stuffing in the center of each piece and brush exposed dough with beaten egg or water, then fold the piece in half so that the edge of the top half does not quite meet the edge of the bottom half. Press and seal tightly with your fingers. Pick up the half-moon shape and wrap it around your finger with the rounded side upward. Press one corner over the other to form a ring; if the corners won't stick together, moisten with egg or water.

WONTONS. Position a 3-inch-square wrapper with a corner toward you. Spread about ½ teaspoon of filling near the corner closest to you. Roll the wrapper around the filling up to the center of the square to enclose filling. Fold the right and left corners to the back of the square so that they overlap, dampen edges with cold water, and firmly press to seal.

Homemade pasta should be used shortly after preparing or allowed to dry completely for later use. With the exception of Asian rice noodles, refrigeration or freezing of fresh pasta does not produce satisfactory results. To dry homemade noodles completely, cut them into desired widths and allow them to dry, uncovered, for about 30 minutes; the pasta should feel dry but still be pliable. Loosely coil a handful of the noodles into a nest shape, then allow the noodle nests to dry completely, at least overnight or as long as several days. Transfer to airtight containers, and store in a cool, dry place for up to 4 months.

Commercially dried pasta and noodles last indefinitely when stored in a cool, dry place. Once a package has been opened, any unused contents should be transferred to an airtight container.

Cooking

Whether cooking fresh or dried pasta or noodles, the essentials are the same: plenty of water; adding the pasta only after the water has reached a rapid boil; stirring to keep the pasta moving; cooking only until barely tender; and draining, saucing, and serving as quickly as possible. Always make sure that the sauce is ready before cooking the pasta, or that it is timed to be ready at the same time the pasta is done. Hot pasta must be eaten as soon as possible; it quickly turns gummy while waiting around for a sauce.

To keep pasta from sticking together during cooking, start with a large pot that has ample space for the pasta to move around from being stirred as well as from the action of the boiling water. Although Italian and Asian cooks frown on the process, a number of American cooks advocate adding about a tablespoon of vegetable or olive oil to the cooking water to further ensure that the pasta will not stick together; I find that oil is not necessary to prevent sticking, but it does seem to help keep the water from boiling over the rim of the pot. Use 4 quarts of water for each pound of pasta. Be sure that the filled pot will not be too heavy to carry to the sink for draining. Generally, it is best to cook no more than 2 pounds of pasta at a time.

Pour the water in the pot, place the pot over high heat, cover to speed up boiling, and bring to a rapid boil. Although generously salting the cooking water definitely adds to the flavor of the cooked pasta, in our age of dietary consciousness, you may wish to reduce the amount of salt or eliminate it altogether. If you decide to add salt, stir it in after the water is boiling, since salted water takes longer to reach a boil. Carefully drop the pasta into the boiling water all at once and stir well to separate the strands. If using long strands of dried pasta, allow the immersed ends to soften before stirring in the remainder. For uniform cooking of all pieces, continue to stir frequently throughout cooking to keep the pasta moving and equally distributed in the water.

Cook pasta until it is al dente, or tender but still firm to the bite. The only way to test for doneness is to quickly remove a piece of the pasta and take a bite. It should be tender but still slightly resilient; there should be no floury taste or uncooked dough in the center. Specific cooking times for fresh pasta are difficult to give due to types of flour and the size, shape, and moisture content of each pasta. The cooking times vary from only 1 to

2 minutes for thin noodles made from all-purpose white flour to 3 to 4 minutes for wider noodles or pasta made from firmer flours; thick shapes and stuffed pastas may take even longer. Dried pasta cooking times also depend on flour type and the size and shape of each pasta; the times range from 3 to 4 minutes for tiny pastas up to 20 minutes for very large pieces; most are ready in 8 to 10 minutes. Refer to the directions on the package label as a starting point, but begin taste testing well before the suggested cooking time to prevent mushy results. When testing for doneness, bear in mind that all pasta continues to cook even after it has been drained.

As soon as the pasta tests almost done, drain it into a colander positioned over a bowl in the sink. The hot water will warm the bowl for tossing pasta with its sauce. Shake the colander a few times to release excess water, discard the water from the bowl, and pour the drained pasta into the warmed bowl. Pour the sauce over the pasta and toss quickly but thoroughly to evenly coat the pasta. Clean the rim of the bowl, add a garnish if desired, transport immediately to the table, and serve as quickly as possible onto preheated plates with a pronged pasta serving utensil (a cross between a fork and a spoon). Or transfer the pasta to preheated plates in the kitchen, garnish, and serve immediately. If you plan to arrange the pasta on top of the sauce on individual plates, toss the pasta in a bit of melted butter or oil, whichever is used in the sauce or is compatible with the sauce ingredients, to prevent the pasta from sticking together. Spoon the sauce onto the preheated plates, add the pasta, garnish it, and serve as fast as you can.

Partially cooked pasta such as lasagna noodles, which will be cooked further during baking, or pasta that will be used in a cold dish should be drained and transferred to a bowl of cold water to halt cooking and keep the pasta from sticking together until called for in the recipe.

When serving dried pasta to a large group, try a restaurant trick: Partially cook the pasta ahead of time, then rinse in cold water to remove the surface starch, toss lightly in flavorless vegetable oil, and set aside in a bowl at room temperature. Just before serving, plunge the pasta into rapidly boiling water to complete the cooking. Drain and sauce as previously described.

COOKING ASIAN NOODLES

Generally speaking, Asians prefer noodles cooked a bit softer than the Western al dente style.

CELLOPHANE NOODLES. Chinese or Southeast Asian transparent noodles (bean threads or silver or shining noodles) are made from mung beans; yam beans are used to make the strongly flavored Japanese counterpart *(shirataki)*. Soak in hot water for 20 to 25 minutes. Drain, then cook for about 3 minutes.

CHINESE EGG NOODLES *(Mein)*. Whether fresh, frozen, or dried, these noodles should be cooked as for pasta. But watch carefully, as they cook in a very short time, often less than 1 minute for thin fresh ones; dried noodles take 6 to 10 minutes.

JAPANESE NOODLES. Cook fresh or dried noodles as for pasta or directly in broth, in which they are usually served. Thick whole-wheat noodles *(udon)* take 12 to 15 minutes, buckwheat noodles *(soba)* are ready in 6 to 7 minutes, and thin noodles *(somen)* cook in 3 to 4 minutes.

RICE STICKS. These wiry dried strands are usually deep-fried in hot fat. They puff up and turn crisp in seconds.

SOUTHEAST ASIAN RICE NOODLES. Whether fresh, frozen, or dried, these noodles should be covered in cold water and soaked for 15 minutes for thin noodles or up to 1 hour for thick ones. Drain and cook briefly as for pasta.

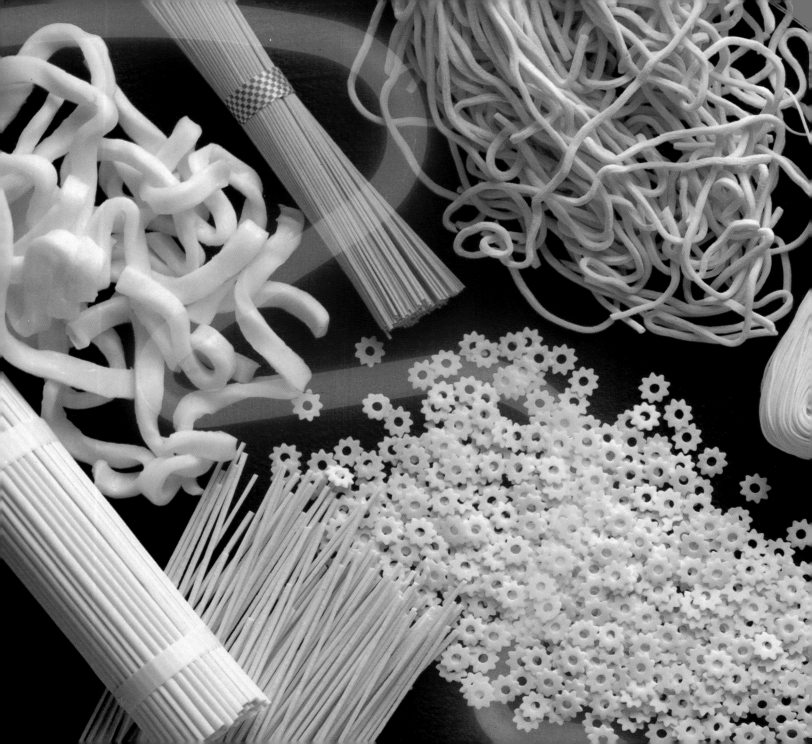

EAST: NOODLES FROM ASIA

Pan-Fried Noodles with Vegetable Beef

1 tablespoon cornstarch
1 tablespoon soy sauce
1 tablespoon rice wine or sherry
1 tablespoon minced or pressed garlic
1 tablespoon minced or pressed fresh
    ginger root
12 ounces tender boneless beef such
    as sirloin, top round, or flank
    steak, trimmed of excess fat and
    sliced into pieces about 2 inches
    long and ½ inch wide
Peanut or other high-quality
    vegetable oil for pan frying and
    stir-frying
1 pound fresh or dried Chinese-style
    egg noodles, cooked until
    tender, then drained and tossed
    with 2 tablespoons soy sauce
4 cups sliced fresh vegetables such as
    asparagus, broccoli, green
    beans, snow peas, or summer
    squash (one kind or a
    combination)
2 tablespoons Chinese oyster sauce
¼ cup sesame seeds, toasted
Whole or julienned Chinese chives or
    green onion tops for garnish

For chow mein, top pan-fried noodles with any favorite stir-fry.

In a bowl, combine the cornstarch, soy sauce, rice wine or sherry, garlic, and ginger root. Add the beef and stir to coat well; set aside for about 15 minutes.

Meanwhile, heat about 2 tablespoons oil in a flat-bottomed sauté pan or skillet, preferably with a nonstick surface. Spread about half of the noodles in the pan and cook, without stirring, over high heat until crisp and evenly golden on the bottom, 4 to 5 minutes. Add a bit more oil around the edges as required to keep noodles from sticking. Slide the noodle cake onto a plate, cover with another plate, invert the cake, and return it to the pan, adding more oil if necessary to prevent sticking. Cook until crisp and golden on the bottom, 2 to 3 minutes. Transfer to a plate and cover with foil to keep warm. Cook the remaining noodles, adding oil as needed. Alternatively, divide the noodles into individual-sized portions and cook separately.

Heat a wok or sauté pan over high heat. Add 2 tablespoons oil and swirl to coat the pan; heat until hot but not smoking. Add the vegetables and stir-fry until crisp-tender, about 2 minutes. Using a slotted utensil, remove vegetables and keep warm. Add 2 tablespoons oil and swirl. Add the reserved beef and stir-fry until browned on all sides, about 2 minutes. Return the vegetables to the pan. Stir in the oyster sauce and stir-fry until the beef and vegetables are heated through and lightly glazed.

To serve, spoon the vegetable beef over the top of each noodle cake. Sprinkle with sesame seeds and garnish with chives or green onion. At the table, cut into wedges and serve.

Serves 8 as part of a meal, or 4 as a main course.

Japanese Noodles in Ginger Broth

For a more complex dish, add cooked seafood or chicken, fresh spinach, julienned green onions, sliced mushrooms, or cubed bean curd (tofu). The *soba* noodles used in my presentation are made with green tea.

In a large pot, bring the water to a rapid boil over high heat. Stir in the salt. Drop in the noodles and cook, stirring frequently, until noodles are tender but still firm to the bite, 6 to 7 minutes for *soba,* or up to 20 minutes for *udon.* Drain, rinse with cold water, and drain again. Set aside.

In a saucepan, combine the stock or broth, ginger root, soy sauce, *mirin* or sherry, and sugar. Bring to a boil over medium-high heat. Reduce the heat to low, cover, and simmer 5 minutes. Strain into a clean saucepan. Place over high heat, add the reserved noodles, and heat through.

To serve, ladle the noodles and broth into preheated bowls, add the pickled ginger and fish cake (if used). Break 1 egg (if used) into each serving. Let stand about 1 minute before serving for residual heat to lightly poach the egg. Sprinkle with seaweed (if used) and serve.

Serves 8 as a soup course, or 4 as a main course.

4 quarts water
1 tablespoon salt
1 pound fresh or dried Japanese buckwheat noodles *(soba)* or thick whole-wheat noodles *(udon)*
2 quarts reconstituted Japanese soup stock *(dashi-no-moto),* homemade light chicken stock, or 2 cups canned chicken broth diluted with 2 cups water
3 tablespoons grated fresh ginger root
2 tablespoons soy sauce, preferably tamari, or to taste
¼ cup sweetened rice wine *(mirin)* or dry sherry
2 teaspoons sugar
Thinly sliced pickled ginger
Sliced fish cake (optional)
8 small chicken eggs or quail eggs (optional)
1 thin sheet dried nori seaweed, lightly toasted over a flame or under a broiler until crisp, shredded or cut into small pieces (optional)

Pan-Fried Dumplings (Potstickers)

Known to the Japanese as *gyōza* and translated from Chinese as "potstickers," these tasty morsels are one of my all-time favorite pasta dishes. Although frequently served browned bottoms up, I prefer to present them with the soft side on top.

In a bowl, combine the pork, onion, cabbage, ginger root, sesame oil, soy sauce, and salt and pepper to taste. Mix well and set aside.

Working with a single sheet of dough at a time (keep the rest covered to prevent drying out), place about 2 teaspoons of the pork mixture just off center and form it into a half circle shape with your fingertips. Moisten the inside edge of the dough with water. Fold the wrapper over the filling so that the edges meet, then pinch the center of the joined edges to adhere. On the side of the dumpling facing you, and beginning just to one side of the pinched center, fold the dough to form 3 little pleats with edges that face toward the center; pinch together at the top to seal tightly. Repeat the pleating on the other side of the pinched center, reversing the folds so that the pleat edges face the center. Leave the back side of the dumpling unpleated.

Heat a skillet over high heat. Add just enough peanut or other vegetable oil to cover the bottom, then swirl the pan to coat bottom and sides. Reduce heat to medium. Add the dumplings, smooth side down, so that they touch each other in straight rows or in a circle. Increase the heat so that the oil sizzles. Cook until the bottoms are browned, then pour in enough stock or broth to come halfway up the sides of the dumplings. Reduce the heat so that the liquid simmers, cover the pot, and cook until the liquid is almost absorbed. Uncover and cook until the bottoms of the dumplings are crisp, adding a bit more oil underneath the dumplings, if necessary. Remove from the heat and, using a spatula, transfer to a plate, and garnish with chives (if used). Serve immediately.

Offer the condiments at the table; each diner mixes ingredients to taste and dips dumpling en route to mouth.

Serves 8 as part of a meal, or 4 as a main course.

10 ounces ground lean pork
1 cup finely chopped onion
1 cup finely chopped napa or other Asian-type cabbage
1 tablespoon minced or grated fresh ginger root
1 tablespoon Asian-style sesame oil
1 tablespoon soy sauce
Salt
Freshly ground black pepper
Asian Wheat Noodles (page 12), cut into 3-inch circles, or about 3 dozen fresh round gyōza or potsticker skins or square wonton wrappers, trimmed into circles (available in Asian markets and some supermarkets)
Peanut or other high-quality vegetable oil for pan frying
About 2 cups homemade chicken stock or canned chicken broth
Chinese chives for garnish (optional)

CONDIMENTS FOR DIPPING
Soy sauce
Rice vinegar or Chinese black vinegar
Asian-style sesame oil
Hot chile oil

Crisp Sweet Thai Noodles
(Mee Krob)

Canola or other high-quality
  vegetable oil for deep-frying
8 ounces dried rice sticks, broken into
  small bunches
4 eggs
6 tablespoons light brown or
  granulated sugar
¼ cup fish sauce *(nam pla)*
¼ cup soy sauce
¼ cup rice vinegar
3 tablespoons freshly squeezed
  lime juice
1 cup finely chopped yellow onion
1 tablespoon minced fresh hot chile
1 tablespoon minced or pressed garlic
12 ounces boned and skinned
  chicken breast, minced
2 green onions, including tops,
  julienned
¼ cup fresh cilantro (coriander)
  leaflets for garnish
Sliced red hot chili for garnish

Fried wiry rice stick threads crowned with sweet and sour syrup are most often served as an appetizer in a Thai meal. Small shrimp, minced pork, or cubed tofu may be substituted for the chicken.

Pour the oil in a wok or deep-fat fryer to a depth of 2 to 3 inches and preheat to about 360° F. Add the rice sticks, a handful at a time, and cook, turning once, until crisp and lightly golden, 12 to 15 seconds. Transfer to paper toweling to drain.

Crack the eggs into a bowl and beat lightly. Hold the bowl about 8 inches over the hot oil; dip a hand into the egg, then stretch it over the surface of the oil to dribble the egg in long threads. Crisscross the oil in several directions to form a thin web of egg over the oil. Cook until lightly golden on the bottom, turn carefully, and cook until egg is golden on the other side. Transfer to paper toweling to drain while repeating the procedure with the remaining egg. After frying all the egg, discard all but about 3 tablespoons of the oil, or transfer that amount to a clean wok or sauté pan.

In a bowl, combine the sugar, fish sauce, soy sauce, vinegar, and lime juice. Set aside.

Heat the oil in the wok or sauté pan over high heat. Add the onion and chile and stir-fry about 1 minute. Add the garlic and reserved fish sauce mixture and cook until the sauce is syrupy, about 2 minutes. Add the chicken and stir-fry until the meat turns opaque, about 2 minutes. Reduce the heat to low and add about one third of the reserved rice sticks and egg threads and gently toss to coat. Add half of the remaining rice sticks and egg and toss, then add the remaining rice sticks and egg and toss until all the rice sticks are coated with syrup.

Transfer to a serving platter, sprinkle with green onion and cilantro, garnish with red chili, and serve immediately.

Serves 6 to 8 as part of a meal.

Thai Fried Noodles *(Pad Thai)*

In Thailand, these noodles are served as a complete lunch or a late supper. If you don't have access to rice noodles, this ancient dish can be made with dried vermicelli; eliminate soaking and cook the pasta until al dente before using. Soybean curd (tofu) may be added along with or substituted for the meat.

As with all stir-frying, assemble the ingredients within arm's reach before heating the wok. Toss gently after adding the noodles to avoid breaking them.

In a bowl, cover the noodles in lukewarm water and let stand to soften, about 15 minutes for fresh noodles or about 30 minutes for dry noodles. Drain and cut into 6-inch lengths, if desired. Set aside.

In a small bowl, combine the fish sauce, vinegar, sugar, and paprika, catsup, or tomato paste. Set aside.

Heat a wok or sauté pan over high heat. Add the oil and swirl to coat the pan. Add the pork or chicken, garlic, and chile and stir-fry for 1 minute. Stir in the drained noodles and the reserved fish sauce mixture and stir-fry about 30 seconds. Push the noodles to one side, pour in about a tablespoon more oil, if necessary, and add the eggs; cook just until slightly set, then break them up. Add the shrimp and stir-fry just until they turn pink. Add most of the bean sprouts, the green onion, and ¼ cup of the peanuts and stir-fry until the sprouts and onions are crisp-tender, 1 to 2 minutes. Remove from the heat and transfer to a serving plate.

Sprinkle with the chopped cilantro, remaining ¼ cup peanuts, and dried shrimp (if used). Garnish with the remaining bean sprouts, cilantro sprigs, and lemon or lime wedges, and serve immediately. Diners squeeze lemon or lime juice to taste.

Serves 8 as a pasta course, or 4 as a main course.

Asian Rice Noodles (page 13), cut about ⅛ inch wide, or 1 pound fresh or dried flat rice noodles
¾ cup fish sauce *(nam pla)*, or 6 tablespoons soy sauce
4 teaspoons rice wine vinegar or distilled white vinegar
2 tablespoons sugar
4 teaspoons high-quality paprika, or ¼ cup catsup or tomato paste
½ cup high-quality vegetable oil, or more if needed
8 ounces boneless pork or boned and skinned chicken, cut into very small pieces
2 tablespoons minced or pressed garlic
2 teaspoons ground dried red hot chile, or 1 tablespoon minced fresh hot chile
4 eggs, lightly beaten
8 ounces medium-sized shrimp, shelled and deveined, tails left intact
10 ounces fresh bean sprouts
3 green onions, including tops, thinly sliced
½ cup chopped unsalted dry-roasted peanuts
¼ cup chopped fresh cilantro (coriander)
Finely minced dried shrimp for garnish (optional)
Fresh cilantro sprigs for garnish
Lemon or lime wedges for garnish

Spicy Mint Noodles

Asian Rice Noodles (page 13), cut
    about ⅛ inch wide, or 1 pound
    fresh or dried rice noodles
½ cup high-quality vegetable oil
3 cups thinly sliced yellow onion
¼ cup julienned fresh red or green
    hot chile or tiny whole fresh
    chiles
1 pound medium-sized shrimp,
    shelled and deveined
2 cups fresh mint leaves
8 ounces fresh bean sprouts
¼ cup fish sauce *(nam pla),* or
    2 tablespoons soy sauce
Fresh mint leaves for garnish
Lime wedges for squeezing

Abundant fresh mint cools the fiery chiles in this quick-and-easy dish inspired by Southeast Asian ingredients. Spaghetti or other thin noodles may be used if you don't want to make rice noodles or if ready-made or dried ones are not available; if you use regular dried pasta, cook it until very al dente and drain before beginning the stir-fry.

In a bowl, cover the rice noodles in lukewarm water and let stand to soften, about 15 minutes for fresh noodles or about 30 minutes for dried noodles. Drain and set aside.

Heat a wok or sauté pan over high heat; add the oil and swirl to coat the bottom and sides of the pan. Add the onion and chiles and stir-fry about 2 minutes. Add the shrimp, the 1 cup mint leaves, drained noodles, and bean sprouts and stir-fry until the shrimp turn bright pink and the sprouts and onions are tender, about 2 minutes. Stir in the fish sauce and heat through.

Garnish with plenty of fresh mint and lime wedges to squeeze at the table. Serve immediately.

Serves 8 as a pasta course, or 4 as a main course.

Vietnamese Spring Rolls (Cha Gio)

DIPPING SAUCE
½ cup fish sauce *(nu'ó'c mâ'm)*, or
    ¼ cup soy sauce, or to taste
¼ cup freshly squeezed lime juice
¼ cup minced or pressed garlic
4 teaspoons sugar, or to taste
1 teaspoon minced fresh red chile
1 teaspoon chili oil, or to taste
1 tablespoon chopped roasted peanuts

**CHICKEN AND SHRIMP
FILLING**
2 ounces dried rice sticks, broken up,
    soaked in hot water for about
    15 minutes, then drained and
    coarsely chopped
8 ounces shelled shrimp, coarsely
    chopped
1 pound finely ground chicken breast
½ cup finely chopped Chinese chives
    or green onions, including tops
¼ cup finely minced carrot
Salt
Freshly ground black pepper

1 pound dried rice paper wrappers,
    about 8 inches in diameter
Water for brushing wrappers
About 24 large, crisp lettuce leaves
About 1 cup fresh cilantro (coriander)
    sprigs
About 1 cup fresh mint leaves
About 1 cup fresh basil leaves,
    preferably Asian type
Oil for deep-fat frying

Pork, beef, or crab are often used in the filling for this popular snack or appetizer.

To make the sauce, combine all ingredients in a bowl and stir until the sugar dissolves. Set aside.

To make the filling, combine all ingredients in a bowl, including salt and pepper to taste, and mix well. Set aside.

Brush each side of several of the rice paper wrappers with water and set aside to soften, about 2 minutes.

Working with one wrapper at a time, spoon a heaping tablespoon of filling onto the lower third of the wrapper, leaving about 1 inch of space along the bottom and sides. Fold the bottom up around the filling, then tuck in each side to encase filling. Continue to roll to form a cylinder. Place seam side down on a lightly oiled baking sheet or platter.

Arrange the lettuce leaves and herbs on a tray or in a shallow container and set on the table. Spoon the Dipping Sauce into small bowls and position at each place.

Pour oil to a depth of 2 inches in a deep-fat fryer or wok and heat to 375° F. Add the rolls, a few at a time, and cook, turning frequently, until golden brown, about 6 minutes. Using a slotted utensil, transfer the rolls to paper toweling to drain while frying the remaining rolls. When all the rolls are cooked, pat with paper toweling to remove excess oil and serve immediately. The rolls may be served whole or sliced into 3 or 4 sections.

To eat, place a few herb sprigs on a lettuce leaf, add a roll, and wrap firmly in the lettuce. Dip into the sauce and enjoy.

Serves 8 as an appetizer, or 4 as a main course.

Golden Threads with Chile Dipping Sauce

In my vegetarian variation on traditional Southeast Asian pork balls, in which meatballs are wrapped in noodles before frying, the noodles themselves form very free-form balls.

To make the dipping sauce, combine all ingredients in a food processor or blender and blend well. Set aside.

In a large pot, bring the water to a rapid boil over high heat. Stir in the 1 tablespoon salt. Drop in the pasta and cook, stirring frequently, until tender but still firm to the bite. Drain.

In a large bowl, toss the pasta with the 2 tablespoons vegetable oil and season to taste with salt and black and cayenne peppers. Stir in the green onion, bamboo shoot or water chestnut, cilantro, and chile. Add the eggs and mix well.

Pour the oil in a deep-fat fryer or deep saucepan to a depth of 2 inches and preheat to 360° F.

Using your hands, form the noodle mixture into balls about the size of golf balls, or larger, if desired; do not compact. Fry the balls, a few at a time, until golden brown, 3 to 4 minutes. The noodles will separate during cooking to form irregular shapes; use a slotted utensil to help keep them intact as much as possible during frying. Transfer to paper toweling, sprinkle with sesame seeds (if used), and drain briefly. Serve hot with the reserved chile sauce and soy sauce for dipping.

Serves 8 as part of a meal, or 4 as a main course.

CHILE DIPPING SAUCE
4 fresh red hot chiles, stemmed
2 garlic cloves, peeled
¼ cup freshly squeezed lime juice
3 tablespoons fish sauce *(nam pla)*, or 2 tablespoons soy sauce
2 tablespoons Asian-style sesame oil

4 quarts water
1 tablespoon salt
Asian Wheat Noodles (page 12) or 1 pound takeout fresh pasta, cut into very thin noodles; or 1 pound thin fresh Asian noodles; or 1 pound dried thin pasta such as *capellini* or *vermicelli*
2 tablespoons high-quality vegetable oil
Salt
Freshly ground black pepper
Ground cayenne pepper
½ cup finely chopped green onion, including green tops
½ cup finely chopped bamboo shoot or water chestnut
¼ cup minced fresh cilantro (coriander)
3 tablespoons minced fresh red hot chile
3 eggs, beaten
Oil for deep-fat frying
Toasted sesame seeds (optional)
Soy sauce for dipping

Afghanistan-Style Leek-Stuffed Pasta with Yogurt and Meat Sauces

Some food historians credit Central and Southwest Asians as the first to stuff noodle dough. The idea spread to China as wontons and potstickers, and then on to Italy as ravioli and other stuffed pastas.

Prepare the meat sauce; add the cinnamon and cumin while simmering.

In a sauté pan or skillet, heat the oil over medium heat. Add the chopped leek and sauté until very tender, about 10 minutes. Season to taste with salt and pepper. Remove from the heat and set aside.

In a bowl, combine the yogurt, garlic, the ¼ cup mint, and salt to taste; set aside.

Prepare the pasta dough as directed and roll out to ¹⁄₁₆ inch thick. Spread half of the pasta on a lightly floured work surface. Mound 1 teaspoon of the filling at 2-inch intervals along the pasta. Brush the exposed dough with the beaten egg, then cover loosely with remaining dough. Press down around filling to force out air and seal dough. Using a pastry wheel or sharp knife, cut between the filling mounds to form 2-inch squares. Set aside on dish towels.

If using wonton wrappers, mound 1 teaspoon of the filling in the center of half of the wrappers. Brush the exposed dough with egg, then cover with the remaining wrappers. Press around the filling to seal. Trim edges with a pastry wheel.

In a large pot, bring the water to a rapid boil over high heat. Stir in the 1 tablespoon salt. Drop in the ravioli and cook, stirring frequently, until tender but still firm to the bite. Drain and toss with the melted butter.

To serve, spoon a portion of the minted yogurt onto each plate. Top with ravioli and drizzle some of the reserved meat sauce over the top. Garnish with leek greens and mint leaves or oregano and serve immediately.

Serves 8 as a pasta course, or 4 as a main course.

½ recipe Bolognese-Style Meat Sauce (page 91)
2 teaspoons ground cinnamon
1½ teaspoons ground cumin
3 tablespoons olive oil, preferably extra-virgin
1½ cups chopped leek, including green portion
Salt
Freshly ground black pepper
2 cups plain yogurt
1 teaspoon minced or pressed garlic
¼ cup minced fresh mint
Basic Pasta (page 8), or 1 pound purchased fresh pasta sheets, or about 48 wonton wrappers (available in most supermarkets)
1 egg, lightly beaten
4 quarts water
1 tablespoon salt
3 tablespoons unsalted butter, melted
Julienned leek, green portion only, for garnish
Fresh mint leaves or oregano for garnish

Indian-Style Sweet Rice Stick Noodles

8 ounces dried rice sticks
½ cup (1 stick) unsalted butter
1 cup almonds, cashews, macadamia
    nuts, or pine nuts
1 cup golden raisins or dried currants,
    plumped in hot water for about
    20 minutes, then drained
2 quarts unsweetened coconut milk
1¼ cups sugar, or to taste
½ teaspoon ground cardamom
4 teaspoons rose water, or to taste
Pesticide-free rose petals for garnish
    (optional)

This unusual dessert from India is also popular among neighboring Southeast Asian countries around the Indian Ocean.

Traditionally, the noodles are simmered in cow's milk; for richer flavor, I've used coconut milk, a popular ingredient of Southeast Asian cuisine. Unsweetened canned coconut milk is available in Asian markets and the ethnic sections of some supermarkets; the best is imported from Thailand. (This is not the very sweet canned cream of coconut sold for tropical drinks.)

To make your own coconut milk, cover 4 cups shredded fresh coconut or dried unsweetened grated coconut (available in natural foods stores) with 6 cups boiling water or warmed milk and let stand for 30 minutes. Strain the liquid through cheesecloth, squeezing the cloth to extract all the liquid.

Break the rice sticks into several clumps in a bowl. Set aside.

In a saucepan, melt the butter over medium heat. Add the nuts and sauté until lightly browned and fragrant, about 4 minutes. Stir in the raisins and sauté about 1 minute longer. Using a slotted utensil, transfer the nuts and raisins to a small bowl and set aside.

Drop the reserved rice sticks into the hot butter and cook, turning continuously, until golden, about 1 minute. Stir in the coconut milk, sugar, and cardamom and bring to a boil. Reduce the heat to low and simmer until the rice sticks are almost tender, about 5 minutes. Stir in the rose water and reserved nuts and raisins. Continue to simmer until the rice sticks are very tender, about 3 minutes.

To serve, ladle into shallow bowls, garnish with rose petals (if used), and serve warm.

Serves 8 to 10 as a dessert.

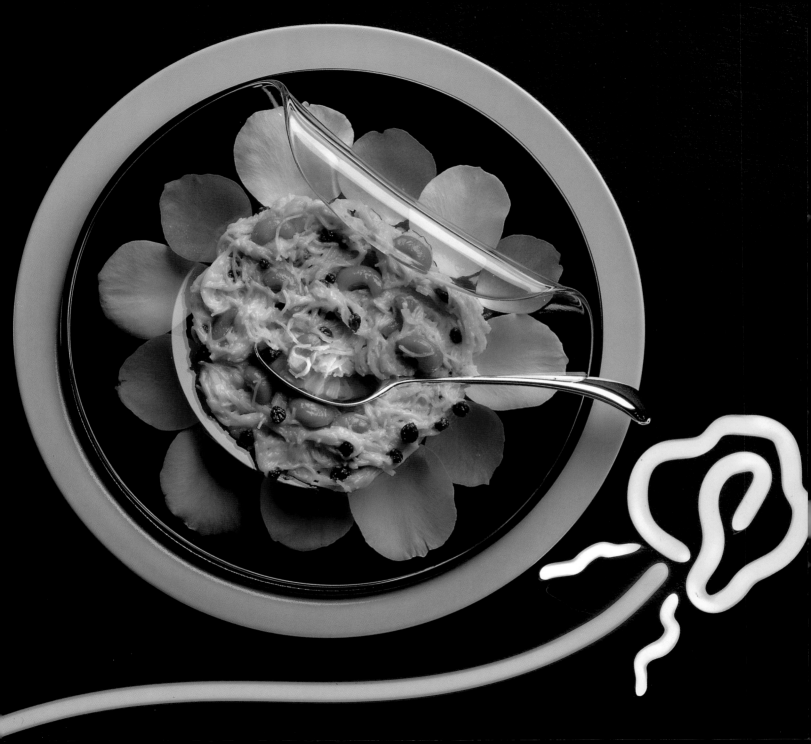

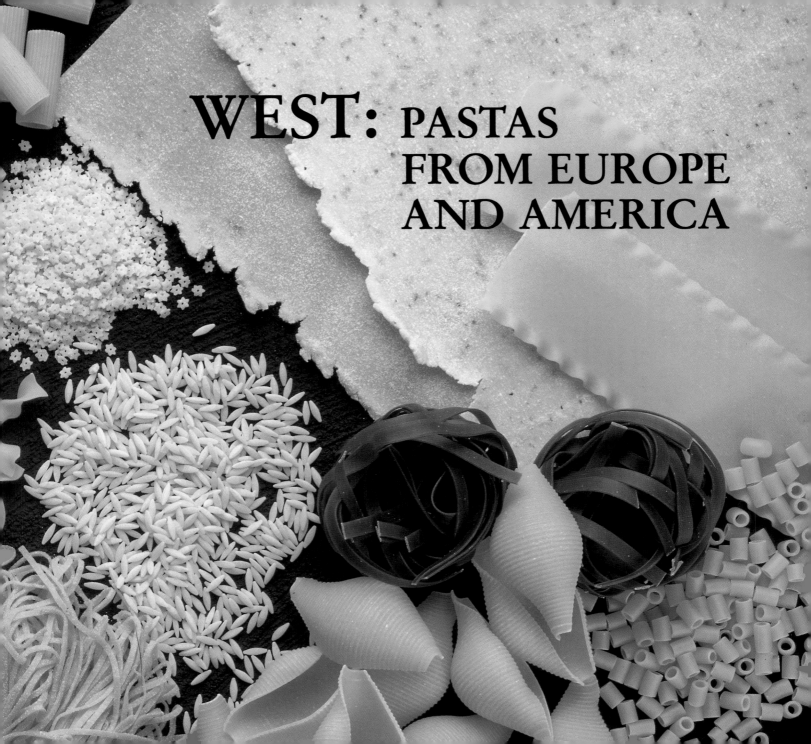

WEST: PASTAS FROM EUROPE AND AMERICA

Wild Mushroom Cappelletti in Broth

Prepare a flavorful stock from duck, chicken, or other fowl in which to cook the cappelletti. The little cap-shaped pasta is also delicious served in a rich cream sauce such as on page 92.

To make the filling, melt the butter in a sauté pan or skillet over medium-high heat. Add the shallots or onion and sauté about 1 minute. Add the mushrooms and sauté until most of the liquid evaporates, about 5 minutes. Stir in the minced thyme, remove from the heat, drain well, and cool to room temperature; then add the egg yolks and salt and pepper to taste and mix well.

Cut the pasta into 2-inch squares. Drop a scant ½ teaspoon of the filling into the center of each square and brush the exposed dough with the beaten egg or water. Diagonally fold the square so that the top corner does not quite meet the bottom corner and press to seal. Pick up the pasta, wrap it around a finger, and press the two outside opposite corners firmly together; moisten corners with egg or water if they won't adhere. The finished form should resemble a peaked bishop's hat.

In a large saucepan, bring the stock to a boil over high heat. Drop in the cappelletti and cook, stirring frequently, until tender but still firm to the bite, about 5 minutes; the pasta should float to the top when ready. Immediately ladle the pasta and stock into preheated bowls, garnish with thyme sprigs, and serve at once. Pass the cheese at the table.

Serves 8 as a soup course, or 4 as a main course.

WILD MUSHROOM FILLING
3 tablespoons unsalted butter
¼ cup minced shallots or red onion
12 ounces wild mushrooms such as chanterelles, morels, or *porcini*, finely chopped
3 teaspoons minced fresh thyme, or 1 teaspoon crumbled dried thyme
2 egg yolks, beaten
Salt
Freshly ground black pepper

Basic Pasta (page 8), or 1 pound takeout fresh pasta sheets
1 egg, lightly beaten
3 quarts homemade poultry stock or canned chicken broth, preferably low-salt type
Fresh thyme sprigs for garnish
Freshly grated Parmesan cheese, preferably Parmigiano-Reggiano, for passing

Garden Pasta Triangles with Herbed Butter

Basic Pasta (page 8), variations (pages 10 and 11), or 1 pound takeout fresh pasta sheets
¾ cup (1½ sticks) unsalted butter, melted
⅓ cup minced mixed fresh herbs
Salt
Freshly ground black or white pepper
4 quarts water
1 tablespoon salt
Yellow cherry tomatoes, cut in half, for garnish
Fresh herb sprigs for garnish
Pesticide-free, nontoxic flowers such as wild mustard or herb blossoms for garnish (optional)
Freshly grated Parmesan cheese, preferably Parmigiano-Reggiano, for sprinkling and passing

In the presentation shown here, I cut triangles from pastas colored and flavored with eight different ingredients—(clockwise from top) purple potato, beet, red sweet pepper, carrot, lime zest, spinach, saffron, and crushed black pepper. For a simpler version use only 1 or 2 different pastas.

Prepare the pasta dough as described and roll out quite thin. Draw a triangle on paper and cut out to use as a template. Lay the pattern on the pasta and cut out with a knife or pastry wheel. Lightly dust pasta triangles with flour and set aside, turning over occasionally, until partially dry, about 20 minutes.

To make the herbed butter, melt the butter in a saucepan over low heat. Remove from the heat and stir in the minced herbs and salt and pepper to taste. Set aside. Reheat just before serving.

In a large pot, bring the water to a boil over high heat. Stir in the 1 tablespoon salt. Add the pasta triangles and cook, stirring frequently, until tender but firm to the bite. Drain, then toss with a little of the herbed butter. Quickly arrange the pasta on preheated plates; drizzle with more of the butter; sprinkle with the tomatoes, herb sprigs, flowers (if used), and cheese; and serve immediately. Pass additional cheese at the table.

Serves 8 as a pasta course, or 4 as a main course.

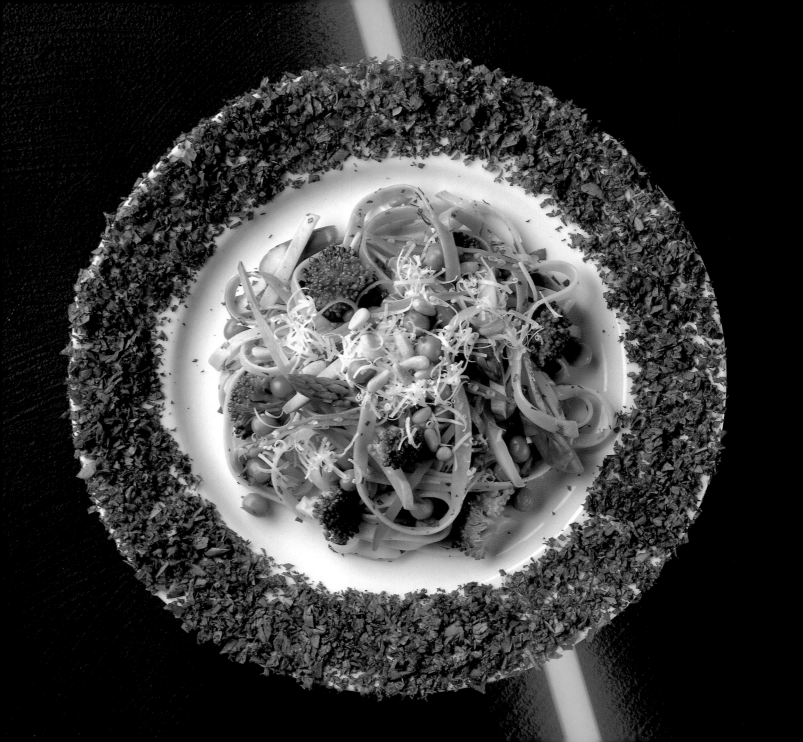

Pasta Primavera

The popularity of this dish, which originated in a New York restaurant, has swept from coast to coast. We now celebrate pasta with fresh vegetables with the same enthusiasm once reserved for Mom and her apple pie. My presentation uses noodles in a variety of pastel colors to add to the springtime quality of the dish; plain egg pasta will taste just as good. For a richer flavor, substitute cream for the olive oil.

Place each green vegetable in a separate bowl. Cover with boiling salted water and let stand until bright green, about 1 minute. Drain into a colander and rinse under cold running water to halt cooking. Set aside.

In a large sauté pan or skillet, heat the oil over low heat. Add the garlic, herbs, and the blanched vegetables. Cook just until heated through. Transfer about half of the mixture to a bowl, cover to keep warm, and set aside.

Meanwhile, in a large pot, bring the stock, water, or diluted broth to a rapid boil. Stir in the 1 tablespoon salt. Drop in the pasta and cook, stirring frequently, until tender but still firm to the bite. Drain, transfer to the pan with the vegetable mixture, and add the ½ cup cheese and salt and pepper to taste. Toss to mix well.

Spoon the pasta onto preheated plates. Sprinkle with the remaining vegetables and the pine nuts. Serve immediately. Offer additional cheese at the table.

Serves 8 as a pasta course, or 4 as a main course.

WINTER VARIATION: Instead of the green vegetables, substitute a mixture of julienned golden and red beets, carrots, turnips or rutabagas, winter squash, or other vegetables. Cook each vegetable separately until it is tender but still holds its shape.

1 pound tender asparagus, cut on the diagonal into 1-inch lengths
1 pound broccoli florets, separated into small pieces
½ pound snow peas or edible-pod peas, julienned
2 cups shelled fresh or thawed frozen green peas
1 pound young zucchini or other green summer squash, cut into lengths the same as snow peas and julienned
Boiling salted water for blanching
½ cup olive oil, preferably extra-virgin
1 tablespoon minced or pressed garlic
½ cup minced mild fresh herbs such as chervil or parsley, preferably flat-leaf type
4 quarts homemade vegetable or chicken stock, water, or 2 quarts canned chicken broth diluted with 2 quarts water
1 tablespoon salt
Basic Pasta (page 8), preferably several vegetable variations (page 10), or 1 pound takeout fresh pasta, cut into thin noodles, or 1 pound dried pasta such as linguini
½ cup freshly grated Parmesan cheese (about 2 ounces), preferably Parmigiano-Reggiano, or crumbled mild goat's milk cheese, plus more for passing
Salt
Freshly ground black pepper
½ cup pine nuts, lightly toasted

Avocado Tomato Pasta

Creative cook Jerry Needle of Manhattan Beach, California, introduced me to the uncooked sauce in this dish after a group of friends had stomped what seemed like tons of grapes with our bare feet as a prelude to Jerry's winemaking. The sauce has since become a new California classic in my summer entertaining. When vine-ripened tomatoes are not in season, or perfectly ripe avocados are unavailable, please choose another recipe.

In a mixing bowl, mash the avocado. Stir in the lime or lemon juice, onion, tomato, chopped basil or cilantro, and salt and pepper to taste.

In a large pot, bring the water to a boil over high heat. Stir in the 1 tablespoon salt. Drop in the pasta and cook until tender but still firm to the bite. Drain and toss in a preheated bowl with the reserved avocado mixture. Garnish with the herb sprigs and cherry tomatoes. Pass the cheese at the table.

Serves 8 as a pasta course, or 4 as a main course.

3 large very ripe avocados, pitted and scooped from peel
3 tablespoons freshly squeezed lime or lemon juice
¾ cup finely chopped red sweet onion
3 cups peeled and chopped ripe tomato
2¼ cups firmly packed fresh basil or cilantro (coriander), chopped
Salt
Freshly ground black pepper
4 quarts water
1 tablespoon salt
Basic Pasta (page 8) or 1 pound takeout fresh pasta, cut into thin noodles, or 1 pound dried pasta such as linguini
Fresh basil or cilantro sprigs for garnish
Cherry tomato quarters for garnish
Freshly grated Parmesan cheese, preferably Parmigiano-Reggiano, for passing

Black Bean Pasta with Corn, Cilantro Cream, and Chile Purée

3 large dried New Mexico or
  California chiles
Herbed Cream (page 92), made with
  cilantro (coriander)
3 tablespoons unsalted butter
¼ cup minced shallots or red onion
1 tablespoon minced fresh green chile
2 cups fresh or thawed frozen corn
  kernels
1 teaspoon ground cumin
Salt
Freshly ground black pepper
Ground dried red hot chile
4 quarts water
1 tablespoon salt
Basic Pasta (page 8), Black Bean
  Variation (page 10), cut into
  triangles or other shapes
2 tablespoons olive oil, preferably
  extra-virgin
Cooked black beans for garnish
Cilantro sprigs for garnish

Fresh pasta laced with puréed black beans is cut into triangles to resemble corn chips in this dish inspired by the foods of the Southwest. For a simpler presentation, cook regular fresh or dried pasta and toss along with the sautéed corn in the cream sauce.

Cover the dried chiles with boiling water and let stand for about 1 hour; reserve liquid. Discard stems and seeds and scrape pulp from inside skins into a food processor or blender. Discard skins and purée the pulp with just enough of the soaking liquid to make a thick paste. Transfer to a squeeze bottle or a plastic bag with a tiny hole cut in a corner. Set aside.

Prepare the cilantro cream and set aside. Reheat just before serving.

Melt the butter in a sauté pan or skillet over medium heat. Add the shallot or onion and minced chile and sauté until soft, about 5 minutes. Add the 2 cups corn, cumin, and salt, pepper, and ground chile to taste. Sauté until the corn is tender, about 3 minutes. Set aside.

In a large pot, bring the water to a rapid boil over high heat. Stir in the 1 tablespoon salt. Drop in the pasta and cook until just tender but still quite firm to the bite. Drain and toss with the oil.

To serve, spoon a pool of the reheated cilantro cream onto each preheated plate. Squirt lines of the chile purée over the sauce, then pull a toothpick or wooden skewer through the sauce to form a design. Top with a portion of the pasta. Add a scoop of the reserved sautéed corn. Sprinkle with the black beans, garnish with cilantro, and serve immediately.

Serves 8 as a pasta course, or 4 as a main course.

Spinach-Stuffed Pasta Packages with Citrus Cream

Citrus Cream (page 92)

SPINACH FILLING
2 tablespoons olive oil, preferably
    extra-virgin
4 ounces thinly sliced prosciutto,
    slivered
1 teaspoon minced or pressed garlic
1 pound fresh spinach leaves, washed,
    drained, tough stems discarded,
    and leaves coarsely chopped
3 tablespoons pine nuts, lightly
    toasted
2 tablespoons golden raisins, plumped
    in hot water for about
    10 minutes, then drained
3 tablespoons unsalted butter
Salt
Freshly ground black pepper

Basic Pasta (page 8), or 1 pound
    takeout fresh pasta sheets
1 egg, lightly beaten
4 quarts water
1 tablespoon salt
Olive oil for brushing cooked pasta
Whole chives blanched in boiling
    water until tender (optional)
Lemon and lime zest for garnish
Freshly grated Parmesan cheese,
    preferably Parmigiano-
    Reggiano, for passing

Here, the Roman-style combination of spinach, prosciutto, pine nuts, and raisins is used as a surprise filling in pasta packets twisted shut at each end. If you have the time, prepare sheets of striped pasta (page 17) from 2 or 3 colors of fresh pasta for the packets; here I've combined spinach and lemon pastas.

For a simpler dish, just stir the sautéed spinach into the cream sauce and toss with noodles or other pasta shapes.

Prepare the Citrus Cream and set aside.

To make the filling, heat the oil in a sauté pan or skillet over medium-high heat. Add the prosciutto and sauté until translucent, about 3 minutes. Add the garlic and sauté 1 minute longer. Add the spinach and sauté until wilted, about 2 minutes. Stir in the pine nuts and raisins, the butter, and salt and pepper to taste. Drain to remove excess liquid and set aside.

Cut the pasta into 24 rectangles about 6 by 4 inches and spread out on a flat surface. Place 1 heaping tablespoon of the Spinach Filling in the center of each piece of pasta, then brush the exposed edges of the pasta with the beaten egg or water. Beginning with a long end, roll the pasta up around the filling and twist each end to seal.

In a large pot, bring the water to a rapid boil over high heat. Stir in the 1 tablespoon salt. Using a slotted utensil, carefully lower the pasta packets into the water and cook, occasionally stirring gently, until the pasta is tender but still firm to the bite. Drain and brush each packet with oil. Tie the ends with chives, if desired.

Meanwhile, reheat the Citrus Cream and spoon a portion onto each plate. Arrange 3 pasta packages on each plate. Garnish with citrus zest and serve immediately. Pass the cheese at the table.

Serves 8 as a pasta course, or 4 as a main course.

Stacked Winter Squash Ravioli with Sage Butter

Traditionally, pumpkin is used to fill ravioli, but I prefer the flavor of 'Buttercup', 'Butternut', 'Delicata', or other winter squash relatives. The filling and sauce also work with traditional stuffed ravioli instead of the larger open version, shown here with squares of spinach pasta and circles of Herb Sprig Pasta (page 10).

To make the filling, melt the butter in a sauté pan or skillet over medium heat. Add the squash and cook, stirring frequently, until very tender. Stir in the cream or half-and-half and cook until the squash is thick and the liquid has evaporated, 45 minutes to 55 minutes. Remove from the heat and season to taste with salt and pepper. Mash with a fork and set aside. Reheat just before using.

To make the Sage Butter, melt the butter in a saucepan over low heat. Stir in the minced sage. Remove from the heat and set aside. Reheat just before serving.

Prepare the pasta dough as directed and roll as thin as possible. Cut the dough into 2 dozen 5-inch squares. Set aside 8 squares. Brush 8 squares with the beaten egg. Place an herb leaf in the center of each of these squares, cover with the 8 remaining pasta pieces, and run each through a hand-cranked pasta machine several times to thin and adhere the pasta. Cut into circles about 4½ inches in diameter.

In a large pot, bring the water to a rapid boil over high heat. Stir in the 1 tablespoon salt. Add the pasta squares and circles and cook until tender but still firm to the bite. Drain and toss with about half of the reheated Sage Butter.

Quickly place the pasta squares on preheated plates and spoon on a portion of the reheated squash filling. Top each with a pasta circle, drizzle with the remaining Sage Butter, garnish with sage leaves, and serve immediately. Pass the cheese at the table.

Serves 8 as a pasta course, or 4 as a main course.

WINTER SQUASH FILLING
¼ cup (½ stick) unsalted butter
2 pounds winter squash, peeled, seeded, and coarsely chopped
1½ cups heavy (whipping) cream, light cream, or half-and-half
Salt
Freshly ground white pepper

SAGE BUTTER
½ cup (1 stick) unsalted butter
¼ cup minced fresh sage leaves, or ¼ cup crumbled dried sage

Basic Pasta (page 8), or 1 pound takeout fresh pasta sheets
1 egg, lightly beaten
Whole fresh sage or other herb leaves or leaflets for pressing between pasta and for garnish
4 quarts water
1 tablespoon salt
Freshly grated Parmesan cheese, preferably Parmigiano-Reggiano, for passing

Pasta with Smothered Onions

ONION SAUCE
½ cup olive oil, preferably extra-
  virgin
4 quarts thinly sliced onions (about
  5 pounds unpeeled)
⅓ cup chopped garlic
Salt
Freshly ground black pepper
1 cup dry red wine
½ cup chopped mixed fresh
  marjoram, summer savory,
  lavender, flat-leaf parsley, and
  thyme, or 3 tablespoons
  crumbled dried *herbes de
  Provence*

4 quarts water
1 tablespoon salt
1 pound dried pasta such as
  orecchiette (little ears)
Fresh herb sprigs (same as used in
  sauce)
Freshly grated Parmesan cheese,
  preferably Parmigiano-
  Reggiano, for passing

One of my favorite cold weather pastas, this dish relies on a simple sauce of onions, cooked until almost caramelized. Any yellow, white, or red onions will do, although I especially enjoy using sweet types when available, such as Vidalia grown in the Deep South, Walla Walla from the Pacific Northwest, or Hawaiian Maui onions.

For a zesty counterpoint, add sautéed spicy sausage slices to the onions along with the wine.

To make the sauce, heat the oil in a large saucepan over medium heat. Add the onions and toss well to coat with oil. Cover, reduce the heat to medium-low, and cook, stirring occasionally, until the onions just begin to color, about 30 minutes.

Remove the cover, add the garlic, increase the heat to medium, and season to taste with salt and a generous amount of pepper. Cook, stirring occasionally, until the onions are almost caramelized, about 25 minutes.

Increase the heat to medium-high, add the wine, and cook until the wine evaporates. Stir in the chopped herb just before tossing the sauce with the pasta.

Meanwhile, bring the water to a rapid boil in a large pot over high heat. Stir in the 1 tablespoon salt. Drop in the pasta and cook, stirring frequently, until tender but still firm to the bite. Drain and transfer to a heated bowl.

Toss the pasta with the sauce, garnish with the herb sprigs, and serve immediately. Pass the cheese at the table.

Serves 8 as a pasta course, or 4 as a main course.

Macaroni with Four Cheeses

4 quarts water
1 tablespoon salt
1 pound dried pasta such as *fusilli* (corkscrews), *penne,* rigatoni, or ziti
6 tablespoons (¾ stick) unsalted butter
½ cup all-purpose flour, preferably unbleached
4 cups milk
2 cups evaporated milk
Salt
Freshly ground black pepper
Freshly grated nutmeg
1½ cups freshly shredded Gruyère cheese (about 5 ounces)
1½ cups freshly shredded Emmenthaler cheese (about 4½ ounces)
1½ cups freshly shredded sharp Cheddar cheese (about 5 ounces)
1 cup freshly grated Parmesan cheese (about 4 ounces), preferably Parmigiano-Reggiano
Pesticide-free, nontoxic flowers such as nasturtiums for garnish (optional)

An American classic is updated with great cheeses.

In a large pot, bring the water to a rapid boil over high heat. Stir in the 1 tablespoon salt. Drop the pasta into the boiling water and cook, stirring frequently, until tender but still firm to the bite. Drain into a colander, rinse under cold running water, drain again, transfer to a large bowl, and set aside.

Preheat an oven to 350° F and grease a 9- by 13-inch baking dish.

In a heavy saucepan, melt the butter over low heat. Whisk in the flour and cook, whisking or stirring almost constantly, until bubbly and fragrant, about 5 minutes; do not brown. Remove from the heat.

Meanwhile, in a saucepan, combine the milk and evaporated milk and bring just to a boil over medium-high heat. Pour all at once into the butter and flour mixture and whisk until smooth. Season to taste with salt, pepper, and nutmeg. Place the pan over medium heat and cook, whisking or stirring constantly, until thickened, about 5 minutes. Pour over the cooked pasta and stir to thoroughly coat the pasta. Spread the pasta evenly in the greased baking dish.

In a bowl, combine the four cheeses, then sprinkle evenly over the pasta. Lightly dust the top with grated nutmeg and bake until the cheese melts and the pasta is heated through, about 25 minutes.

Meanwhile, preheat a broiler.

Place the baking dish under the broiler and cook until the cheese is slightly golden, about 3 minutes. Garnish with flowers (if used). Serve immediately.

Serves 8 as a pasta course, or 4 as a main course.

Bacon and Tomato Pasta

According to Hollywood set designer Joe Bevacqua, this is Sophia Loren's favorite pasta dish. Surprisingly, it is made with American-style smoked bacon and dried pasta; it's too hearty for delicate fresh noodles.

Place the bacon in a sauté pan or skillet over medium-low heat and cook until done but not crisp. Add the onion and cook, stirring frequently, until onion is soft and lightly golden, about 5 minutes.

Combine the tomatoes and ½ cup of the chopped basil in a food processor or blender and coarsely purée. Transfer to the bacon and onion mixture. Increase the heat to medium-high and bring to a boil. Reduce the heat to low and simmer for about 30 minutes.

In a large pot, bring the water to a rapid boil. Stir in the salt. Drop in the pasta and cook until tender but still firm to the bite. Drain.

Meanwhile, drizzle the heavy cream into the simmering sauce, then add the remaining ½ cup chopped basil. Heat through, then toss with the drained pasta, garnish with the basil sprigs, and serve immediately. Pass the cheese at the table.

Serves 6 to 8 as a pasta course, or 4 as a main course.

½ pound smoked bacon, cut into 1-inch lengths
1 cup finely chopped yellow onion
2 cups peeled, seeded, and chopped fresh or drained canned tomatoes
1 cup packed chopped fresh basil
4 quarts water
1 tablespoon salt
1 pound dried pasta such as *penne* or *rigatoni*
½ cup heavy (whipping) cream
Fresh basil sprigs for garnish
Freshly grated Parmesan cheese, preferably Parmigiano-Reggiano, for passing

Pasta Ribbons with Peas and Prosciutto Cream

PEAS AND PROSCIUTTO CREAM
½ cup (1 stick) unsalted butter
4 ounces prosciutto or flavorful baked
    ham, sliced (not too thin) and
    cut into julienne
1 cup shelled fresh or thawed frozen
    tiny peas
½ cup heavy (whipping) cream
1 cup freshly grated Parmesan cheese
    (about 4 ounces), preferably
    Parmigiano-Reggiano
Salt
Freshly ground white pepper
Freshly ground nutmeg

4 quarts water
1 tablespoon salt
Basic Pasta (page 8) or 1 pound
    takeout fresh pasta, cut into
    3-inch-wide ribbons
¼ cup (½ stick) unsalted butter,
    melted
Cooked tiny peas for garnish
Parmigiano, preferably Parmigiano-
    Reggiano, for passing

The sauce in this recipe has been a longtime favorite in my kitchen. It is equally delicious simply tossed with cooked fresh or dried noodles.

For the presentation shown here, prepare equal portions of fresh pasta flavored with puréed red sweet pepper, carrot, and spinach. Cut into ¼-inch-wide noodles, then moisten the edges and arrange strips together in alternating colors. Press with your fingertips to seal. Alternatively, lightly brush a wide strip of one of the pastas with water, overlay with noodles of the other colors to form stripes, and press with your fingertips to seal. In either case, dust pasta lightly with flour and run it through a hand-cranked pasta machine 2 or 3 times to bind the colors together into a wide ribbon.

To make the sauce, melt the butter in a sauté pan or skillet over medium heat. Add the prosciutto and cook until translucent, about 5 minutes. Add the peas and continue cooking until peas are crisp-tender, about 2 minutes. Stir in the cream, the 1 cup cheese, and salt, pepper, and nutmeg to taste. Reduce the heat to low, and heat through; do not allow to boil.

In a large pot, bring the water to a rapid boil over high heat. Stir in the 1 tablespoon salt. Drop in the pasta and cook, stirring frequently, until tender but still firm to the bite. Drain well, then toss with the melted butter.

To serve, spoon a portion of the sauce onto each plate and fold 1 or 2 ribbons so that they overlap on top of the sauce. Sprinkle with the peas and serve immediately. Pass cheese at the table.

Serves 8 as a pasta course, or 4 as a main course.

Beet Pasta with Pork and Creamy Blue Cheese

Look for dried beet pasta in interesting shapes, or use freshly made pasta and cut it into geometric or fanciful shapes.

To toast the walnuts, preheat an oven to 350° F. Spread the nuts in a shallow ovenproof pan and place in the oven, stirring occasionally, until lightly toasted and fragrant. Transfer to a plate and let cool; coarsely chop and set aside.

Bake, microwave, steam, or boil the beets until tender. Cool slightly, peel, and cut into julienne. Set aside.

In a sauté pan or skillet, heat the oil over medium heat. Add the onion and sauté until soft and lightly golden, about 8 minutes. Add the garlic and pork and sauté until the pork is lightly browned and just past the pink stage inside, about 3 minutes. Stir in the cream or half-and-half and the cheese and cook, stirring continuously, until the cheese melts and the sauce is the consistency of thickened cream. Season to taste with salt and pepper. Remove from the heat and set aside; reheat just before serving.

In a large pot, bring the water to a rapid boil over high heat. Stir in the 1 tablespoon salt. Drop in the pasta and cook, stirring frequently, until tender but still firm to the bite. Drain and transfer to a heated bowl. Add the reheated sauce and half of the walnuts and toss to coat the pasta. Add the beets and toss gently. Sprinkle with the remaining walnuts, garnish with beet greens, and serve immediately.

Serves 8 as a pasta course, or 4 as a main course.

1 cup walnuts
½ pound red or golden beets, unpeeled
¼ cup walnut or olive oil, preferably extra-virgin
½ cup finely chopped red onion
1 teaspoon minced or pressed garlic
8 ounces boneless lean pork, cut into bite-sized pieces
2 cups heavy (whipping) cream, light cream, or half-and-half
10 ounces Gorgonzola or other creamy blue cheese, crumbled
Salt
Freshly ground black pepper
4 quarts water
1 tablespoon salt
Basic Pasta (page 8), Vegetable Variation (page 11) made with beets, or 1 pound beet-flavored takeout fresh pasta, cut into wide strips and pinched in the center to form bowtie shapes, or 1 pound dried beet-flavored pasta
Small whole beet greens for garnish

Pasta Carbonara

The picturesque name of this Roman dish translates as "charcoal-maker's pasta"; the hearty sauce was a particular favorite among coal workers. I've tasted numerous versions over the years but prefer this creamy one made without onions.

In a large pot, bring the water to a rapid boil over high heat. Stir in the 1 tablespoon salt.

To begin the sauce, heat 2 tablespoons of the oil in a sauté pan or skillet over medium heat. Add the *pancetta* and cook until the meat is translucent, about 5 minutes. Reduce the heat to low, add the butter, and simmer until the butter melts. Remove from the heat and set aside.

Drop the pasta into the boiling water and cook, stirring frequently, until tender but still firm to the bite.

Meanwhile, in a large bowl, combine the egg yolks, the remaining 2 tablespoons oil, the 1½ cups cheese, the cream, and salt and a generous amount of pepper to taste. Stir in the cooled *pancetta* and butter.

Drain the pasta and turn into the bowl with the sauce. Toss well, sprinkle with the parsley, and serve immediately. Pass additional cheese at the table.

Serves 8 as a pasta course, or 4 as a main course.

4 quarts water
1 tablespoon salt
¼ cup olive oil, preferably extra-virgin
2 cups (about 10 ounces) diced *pancetta* (Italian bacon)
¼ cup (½ stick) unsalted butter
Basic Pasta (page 8) or 1 pound fresh pasta, cut into thin noodles, or 1 pound dried pasta such as spaghettini
6 egg yolks, at room temperature
1½ cups freshly grated Parmesan cheese (about 4 ounces), preferably Parmigiano-Reggiano, plus more for passing
¾ cup heavy (whipping) cream
Salt
Freshly ground black pepper
¼ cup minced parsley, preferably flat-leaf type

Chicken-Pistachio Neon Ravioli with Saffron Sauce

A dramatic presentation updates an ancient favorite. For the photograph, I cooked a few dried lasagna noodles in water tinted with a generous amount of blue food color paste, then I cut off and used only the curly edges as a garnish. If the brilliant hues are too shocking for your taste, use the filling to stuff any fresh pasta dough.

To make the filling, melt the butter in a sauté pan or skillet over medium heat. Add the shallot or leek and sauté until soft, about 5 minutes. Add the chicken and nuts and sauté until chicken is opaque, about 3 minutes. Cool to room temperature, then place in a food processor and finely chop. Transfer to a bowl, stir in the herb, egg yolks, minced truffle (if used), and salt and pepper to taste. Cover and chill for 30 minutes.

Prepare the Saffron Sauce and set aside.

Divide the ingredients for the pasta dough into 3 equal portions. Prepare each portion as described, adding a generous amount of a food color paste to each portion. Roll out until quite thin and cut 1 color dough into matching pairs of circles about 2½ inches in diameter. Cut 1 of the remaining doughs into triangles and the other into squares the same size as the circles. On half of the pasta pieces, place a rounded teaspoon of the filling. Brush the dough all around the filling with the beaten egg or water, cover with the matching second shape, and press down firmly around the mounds of filling to seal the pasta. Set aside on a dish towel.

In a large pot, bring the water to a rapid boil over high heat. Stir in the 1 tablespoon salt. Add the round ravioli and cook, stirring frequently, until tender but firm to the bite. Drain and toss with some of the melted butter. Cook, drain, and toss each remaining ravioli color separately.

Meanwhile, reheat the sauce and spoon a portion onto 8 preheated plates. Top with 1 of each color ravioli. Sprinkle the saffron threads (if used) over the sauce and garnish with a truffle slice (if used).

Serves 8 as a pasta course, or 4 as a main course.

CHICKEN-PISTACHIO FILLING
3 tablespoons unsalted butter
⅓ cup chopped shallot or leek
12 ounces boned and skinned chicken breast, chopped
⅓ cup coarsely chopped pistachios
3 tablespoons minced fresh summer savory, marjoram, or parsley
4 egg yolks
Minced fresh truffle (optional)
Salt
Freshly ground black pepper

Saffron Sauce (page 93)
Basic Pasta (page 8)
3 different food color pastes
1 egg, lightly beaten
4 quarts water
1 tablespoon salt
¼ cup (½ stick) unsalted butter, melted
Saffron threads for garnish (optional)
Sliced fresh truffle for garnish (optional)

Duck Lasagna

Bolognese-Style Meat Sauce (page 91)
3 tablespoons olive oil, preferably extra-virgin
1 duck (about 5 pounds), cut into pieces, excess fat removed
White Sauce (page 90)
4 quarts water
1 tablespoon salt
Basic Pasta (page 8) or 1 pound takeout fresh pasta sheets, cut into strips about 5 by 10 inches, or 1 pound dried lasagna noodles
2 cups freshly grated Parmesan cheese (about 8 ounces), preferably Parmigiano-Reggiano
¼ cup (½ stick) unsalted butter

This was standard takeout fare at my Twin Peaks Grocery a decade ago.

Prepare the meat sauce and simmer for 1 hour. Meanwhile, heat the oil in a sauté pan or skillet over medium-high heat. Add the duck and brown all over. Wrap the duck in cheesecloth and immerse in the meat sauce. Continue to simmer, turning the duck several times, until the duck is very tender, about 2 hours. Transfer the duck to a plate to cool, then remove the cheesecloth. Discard skin and bones; shred duck meat and return it to the simmering meat sauce.

Meanwhile, prepare the White Sauce as described and set aside.

In a large pot, bring the water to a rapid boil. Stir in the salt. Add the noodles, a few at a time, and cook just until barely tender. Using a slotted utensil, remove the noodles to drain. Rinse each noodle under cold running water, then squeeze them with your hands and lay them on a cloth dish towel (noodles will stick to paper). Pat dry with another cloth towel.

Preheat an oven to 450° F and grease the bottom and sides of a 12- by 9-inch baking pan, preferably with straight sides and square corners.

To assemble, spread a thin layer of the meat sauce on the bottom of the pan. Add a single layer of noodles to completely cover the bottom of the pan; fill any holes in the pasta layer with trimmings. Spread a thin layer of the meat sauce over the noodles, cover with a thin layer of the White Sauce, then lightly sprinkle with the cheese. Continue layering in this way until all the ingredients have been used, ending with a layer of White Sauce and a sprinkling of cheese. Dot with the butter and bake until the top forms a lightly golden crust, about 15 minutes. Remove from the oven and let stand about 10 minutes before cutting into squares and serving.

Serves 8 as a pasta course, or 4 as a main course.

Salmon-Stuffed Black Pasta Roll with Roasted Red Pepper Sauce

Be sure ingredients for the filling are well chilled before preparing and do not let the pasta dry very long before rolling. Vary this technique with any color pasta and a favorite filling.

To make the sauce, roast the peppers over charcoal or a gas flame or place under a broiler, turning several times, until the skin is charred all over. Place in a loosely closed paper bag to cool for about 10 minutes. Rub away charred skin with your fingertips. Cut peppers in half; seed, devein, and coarsely chop.

In a saucepan, combine the peppers and the 4 cups cream over medium heat and cook until the cream is reduced by half, 10 to 15 minutes. Transfer to a food processor or blender and purée until smooth. Season to taste with salt and cayenne pepper. Set aside. Reheat just before serving.

To make the filling, purée the salmon in a food processor or blender until as smooth as possible. Add salt and pepper to taste, and the eggs. Blend until well mixed. With the motor running, slowly add the 1 cup plus 2 tablespoons cream and purée until very smooth.

With a sharp knife, trim the edges of the pasta straight. Evenly spread the filling over each pasta sheet, tapering off toward the edges. Starting on a long side, roll up each pasta sheet jelly-roll fashion. Wrap in a double layer of cheesecloth and tie with cotton string in several places.

In a wide pan, bring to a simmer enough water to cover the pasta rolls. Add the rolls and simmer for 20 minutes. Transfer the rolls to a wire rack set over a tray to drain and rest for about 10 minutes. Unwrap the pasta and cut into 1-inch-wide slices; rinse knife between each cut to prevent pasta color from bleeding onto the filling.

To serve, spoon a pool of the reheated sauce onto each preheated plate. Top with 2 to 4 slices of pasta roll and garnish with sweet pepper and caviar (if used). Serve immediately.

Serves 8 as a pasta course, or 4 as a main course.

ROASTED RED PEPPER SAUCE
6 red sweet peppers
4 cups heavy (whipping) cream
Salt
Ground cayenne pepper

SALMON FILLING
10 ounces fresh salmon fillet
Salt
Freshly ground white pepper
2 eggs
1 cup plus 2 tablespoons heavy (whipping) cream

Basic Pasta (page 8), preferably Squid-Ink Variation (page 11), rolled out into 2 rectangles about 15 by 8 inches, or 2 takeout fresh pasta sheets
Water
Sweet red pepper cut into interesting shapes for garnish
Fresh caviar for garnish (optional)

Lobster Pasta

POACHED LOBSTER
2 gallons water
2 celery stalks, chopped
1 onion, quartered
3 or 4 fresh parsley sprigs
2 bay leaves
2 live Maine lobsters (about
    1½ pounds *each*)

LOBSTER SAUCE
¼ cup (½ stick) unsalted butter
2 cups *each* chopped leek, celery, and
    carrot
1½ cups chopped tomato
¾ cup chopped red sweet pepper
1 bay leaf
¼ cup chopped fresh tarragon
1½ cups dry white wine
2 cups heavy (whipping) cream
3 tablespoons dry sherry
1 vanilla bean
Salt
Freshly ground white pepper

4 quarts water
1 tablespoon salt
Basic Pasta (page 8) or 1 pound
    takeout fresh pasta, cut into
    thin noodles, or 1 pound dried
    pasta shells or other fanciful
    shapes
Blanched julienned leek, carrot, and
    sweet red pepper for garnish
Fresh tarragon sprigs for garnish

If you have the time, prepare the fresh Ginger Pasta on page 11 for this special occasion dish.

To cook the lobster, combine the water, celery, onion, parsley, and bay leaves in a large pot and bring to a boil over high heat. Drop the lobsters head first into the boiling water and cook until the shells turn bright red and the meat is opaque, about 8 minutes. Remove the lobsters, drain, and set aside until cool enough to handle; reserve the poaching liquid. Break the lobster tail off from each body. Using scissors, cut a lengthwise slit along the soft underpart of the tail, remove and set aside the meat and all shell pieces; discard the vein that runs along the back. Crack the claws, carefully remove the meat intact, and set aside. Discard the greenish tomalley (liver) from the lobster body and set aside any coral-colored roe that may be found in female lobsters. Coarsely chop all pieces of the lobster shell and set aside.

To make the sauce, melt the butter in a large sauté pan or saucepan over medium heat. Add the chopped leek, celery, and carrot and sauté until the vegetables are soft, about 5 minutes. Add the reserved lobster shells and sauté about 4 minutes longer. Stir in the tomato, sweet pepper, bay leaf, tarragon, wine, and 4 cups of the reserved poaching liquid. Bring to a boil, then reduce the heat to low and simmer for 20 minutes. Strain through a fine wire sieve into a clean saucepan and bring to a boil over medium-high heat. Cook until the liquid is reduced by half. Stir in the cream, sherry, and vanilla bean, reduce the heat to medium-low, and cook, stirring frequently, until the sauce is reduced to about 4 cups; it should be about the consistency of heavy cream. Slice the reserved lobster tail meat and stir it into the sauce to heat through. Season to taste with salt and pepper and set aside. Just before serving remove the vanilla bean and reheat the sauce.

Meanwhile, in a large pot, bring the 4 quarts water to a boil over high heat. Stir in the 1 tablespoon salt. Add the pasta and cook, stirring frequently, until tender but firm to the bite. Drain and toss with the reheated sauce. Arrange on preheated plates and garnish with the julienned vegetables, reserved lobster claw meat and roe, and tarragon and serve immediately.

Serves 8 as a pasta course, or 4 as a main course.

Spanish Pasta with Shellfish (*Fideuá*)

½ cup olive oil, preferably extra-virgin, or more as needed for sautéing
1 pound medium-sized shrimp, shelled and deveined
1 pound cleaned squid, sliced into rings, tentacles separated
½ cup chopped shallots or red onion
1 pound dried spaghetti or other thin pasta, broken into 3-inch lengths
2 tablespoons minced or pressed garlic
1 cup peeled, seeded, and chopped fresh or drained canned tomato
3 quarts homemade fish or chicken stock or canned chicken broth
1 teaspoon crumbled saffron threads
Salt
Ground cayenne pepper
½ cup sliced pitted flavorful green olives
About 24 mussels or clams, or a combination
Roasted red sweet pepper, cut into strips, for garnish
Fresh herb sprigs such as marjoram or flat-leaf parsley for garnish
Lemon wedges for squeezing

An unusual pasta dish, *fideuá* is a near relative of traditional paella.

In a paella pan or large sauté pan, heat the oil over medium-high heat. Add the shrimp and sauté until they turn bright pink. Remove shrimp with a slotted utensil and set aside. Add the squid and sauté until opaque, about 1 minute. Remove squid with a slotted utensil and set aside.

Add the shallots or onion to the pan and sauté about 3 minutes. Add the pasta and sauté until golden, about 5 minutes. Add the garlic and tomato and sauté about 1 minute longer. Stir in the stock or broth, saffron, and salt and cayenne to taste and bring to a boil. Cook, stirring almost continuously, until the pasta is almost tender and only a little liquid remains, about 20 minutes.

Stir the olives into the pasta, then arrange the mussels or clams and the reserved shrimp and squid over the pasta. Reduce the heat to low, cover, and cook until the liquid is absorbed and the pasta begins to crust around the edges, 6 to 8 minutes.

Remove from the heat and let stand about 5 minutes before serving. Garnish with sweet pepper strips and herb sprigs. Offer lemon to squeeze over the top at the table.

Serves 8 as a pasta course, or 4 as a main course.

Poppyseed Noodles with Butterscotch Apples

Instead of starting a meal with pasta, turn the tables and end with these lightly sweetened noodles. When the apples are cooked with honey instead of brown sugar, this makes an interesting side dish with roast pork or lamb.

To make the Butterscotch Apples, melt the butter in a sauté pan or skillet over medium heat. Add the apple slices, cinnamon, nuts, poppy seeds, and drained currants or raisins and sauté until the apples are lightly browned.

In a saucepan, combine the cream or half-and-half and the brown sugar over low heat and simmer, stirring, until the brown sugar is completely dissolved, 4 to 5 minutes. Pour over the apples and simmer until the apples are tender but still hold their shape and the cream is slightly thickened.

Meanwhile, in a large pot, bring the water to a rapid boil. Stir in the salt. Drop in the pasta and cook, stirring frequently, until tender but still firm to the bite. Drain and transfer to a heated bowl. Pour the Butterscotch Apples over the pasta and gently toss to coat well.

To serve, spoon onto preheated plates, garnish with flowers (if used), and serve immediately.

Serves 8 as a dessert pasta or side dish.

BUTTERSCOTCH APPLES
½ cup (1 stick) unsalted butter
4 large apples, peeled, cored, and
    thinly sliced
2 teaspoons ground cinnamon
1 cup chopped pecans or walnuts
3 tablespoons poppy seeds
½ cup dried currants or raisins,
    plumped in cognac or hot water
    for 20 minutes, then drained
1 cup heavy (whipping) cream, light
    cream, or half-and-half
1 cup packed light brown sugar

4 quarts water
1 tablespoon salt
Basic Pasta (page 8), Seeded Variation
    (page 11) made with poppy seeds
    and ½ cup powdered sugar
    added to flour, cut into noodles
    about 1 inch wide
Pesticide-free, nontoxic flowers such
    as dianthus (pinks), violas, or
    violets for garnish (optional)

Fried Coffee-Pasta Nests

Basic Pasta (page 8), Coffee Variation
(page 10) made with ½ cup
powdered sugar added to flour
High-quality vegetable oil for deep-
fat frying
2 cups honey
¼ cup cognac
1 cup chopped pistachios or almonds
Rich coffee or vanilla ice cream
Fresh mint or scented geranium
sprigs or leaves for garnish

For variety try this unusual dessert with Chocolate Pasta (page 10) and chocolate ice cream.

Prepare the pasta as directed, roll to about 1/16 inch thick, and cut into thin noodles. While the noodles are still moist and pliable, divide them into 6 portions, and form each portion into a nest.

Meanwhile, pour the oil to a depth of 2 inches in a deep-fat fryer and preheat to about 365° F. Position a nest in overlapping wire baskets with long handles (sold in cookware stores) or in a wire strainer. Carefully lower the basket or strainer into the oil and hold it in position until the pasta is crisp and lightly golden, 2 to 3 minutes. Transfer the nest, bottom side up, to paper toweling to drain while the other nests are fried. (This can be done 3 to 4 hours in advance of serving.)

In a saucepan, combine the honey and cognac over low heat. Cook, stirring almost continuously, until the honey comes to a boil. Reduce the heat to low and simmer for about 2 minutes. Remove from the heat and cool to lukewarm.

Just before serving, invert the nests and place them on plates. Sprinkle each nest with some of the nuts and spoon the honey mixture over the top to coat the nests. Add a scoop of ice cream in the center, sprinkle with the remaining nuts, garnish with mint or scented geranium, and serve immediately.

Serves 6 as a dessert.

Sweet-Cheese Peppermint Ravioli with Chocolate Sauce

SWEET-CHEESE FILLING
14 ounces *mascarpone* or cream
    cheese, at room temperature
2 tablespoons sugar, or to taste
1 egg yolk

CHOCOLATE SAUCE
8 ounces semisweet or bittersweet
    chocolate, chopped
2 tablespoons unsalted butter
1 cup heavy (whipping) cream
1 teaspoon vanilla extract

Basic Pasta (page 8), Flavored-Oil
    Variation (page 10) made with
    peppermint oil added to eggs
    and ½ cup powdered sugar
    added to flour
Red or bright pink food color paste
1 egg, lightly beaten
4 quarts water
3 tablespoons unsalted butter, melted
Multicolored confectionery sprinkles
    for garnish (optional)

This dessert is outrageous in both appearance and taste!

To make the filling, combine the cheese, sugar, and egg yolk in a bowl. Set aside.

To make the sauce, combine the chocolate, butter, and cream in a saucepan over low heat or in a bowl in a microwave oven at half power. Cook, stirring frequently, until the chocolate is melted and the mixture is smooth. Stir in the vanilla and cool to room temperature. Set aside. Slowly reheat just before serving.

Prepare the pasta as directed, add food color, and knead until streaked with color; do not overmix color. Roll out as thinly as possible and cut into 5-inch squares. Mound about 3 tablespoons of the filling in the center of half of the squares. Brush the exposed dough around the filling with the beaten egg. Cover each with the remaining pasta squares and press around the filling to eliminate air and seal. Cut with cookie cutters into fanciful shapes, or trim edges with a fluted pastry wheel.

In a large pot, bring the water to a rapid boil over high heat. Add the ravioli, a few at a time, and cook until tender but still firm to the bite. Using a slotted utensil, remove the ravioli to a platter. Lightly brush with the melted butter.

To serve, ladle a pool of the reheated sauce onto preheated plates, top with a ravioli, and sprinkle with confectionery sprinkles (if used). Serve immediately.

Serves 8 as a dessert.

SOME BASIC SAUCES

Tomato Sauce

When flavorful summer tomatoes are plentiful, make this simple Italian classic in quantity and freeze for use as is on pasta or in recipes calling for an all-purpose tomato sauce. Whenever good tomatoes are scarce, canned plum tomatoes make much better sauce than out-of-season supermarket varieties.

Minced fresh or crumbled dried herbs may be added for variety, as can ground or crushed dried red hot chile.

½ cup olive oil, preferably extra-
    virgin
1 cup finely chopped onion
1 cup finely chopped carrot
1 cup finely chopped celery
2 teaspoons minced or pressed
    garlic, or to taste
4 cups peeled and chopped fresh or
    drained canned plum
    tomatoes
Salt

In a saucepan, heat the oil over medium-high heat. Add the onion, carrot, and celery and sauté until soft and lightly golden, about 5 minutes. Add the garlic and sauté 1 minute longer. Stir in the tomatoes and salt to taste. Reduce the heat to low and simmer until thick, about 30 minutes. Use immediately, or cover and refrigerate for up to 4 or 5 days. Reheat before using.

For a smoother sauce, transfer to a food processor or blender and purée. Pour into a clean pan and reheat before using.

Makes about 4 cups.

White Sauce

Whether you call it French béchamel, Italian *balsamella,* or plain old American white sauce, this smooth concoction is a basic component of lasagne and cannelloni. Try it on its own as a rich-tasting pasta sauce with less fat than cream-based toppings; of course, lots of added cheese makes it even more wonderful.

5 tablespoons unsalted butter
5 tablespoons all-purpose flour
3 cups milk
Salt
Freshly ground white pepper
Freshly grated nutmeg (optional)

In a heavy saucepan, melt the butter over low heat. Add the flour and whisk briskly to blend until smooth; do not brown. Add the milk all at once and whisk until very smooth. Season to taste with salt, pepper, and nutmeg (if used). Simmer, stirring frequently, until thickened to the consistency of heavy cream, about 10 minutes. Use immediately, or cover and set aside for up to 2 hours and slowly reheat before using.

Makes about 3 cups.

Bolognese-Style Meat Sauce

Every book on pasta needs to include this classic sauce, which is marvelous over fresh noodles or just about any dried pasta and as a filling in lasagna or other stuffed pastas.

⅓ cup olive oil, preferably extra-virgin
6 tablespoons (¾ stick) unsalted butter
⅓ cup chopped onion
⅓ cup chopped carrot
⅓ cup chopped celery
1½ pounds ground lean beef, chopped a second time in a food processor or grinder
2 cups dry white wine
1 cup milk
4 ounces chicken livers (about 4), very finely chopped (optional)
2 bay leaves
1 tablespoon minced fresh thyme, or 1 teaspoon crumbled dried thyme
4 cups peeled and chopped fresh or undrained canned plum tomatoes
¼ teaspoon freshly grated nutmeg, or to taste
Salt
Freshly ground black pepper

Heat the oil and butter in a large, heavy saucepan over medium heat. Add the onion, carrot, and celery and sauté until soft, about 5 minutes. Add the ground beef, breaking it up with a wooden spoon, and cook until it just loses its pinkness; do not brown.

Increase the heat to medium-high; add the wine and cook, stirring frequently, until the wine evaporates. Add the milk, chicken livers (if used), bay leaves, and thyme. Reduce the heat to medium and cook, stirring frequently, until the milk evaporates. Stir in the tomatoes and bring almost to a boil, then reduce the heat to very low, stir in the nutmeg and salt and pepper to taste, and simmer until very tender and flavorful, 4 to 5 hours. Use immediately, or cool slightly, then cover and refrigerate for up to 4 or 5 days. Reheat before serving.

Makes about 4 cups.

Fresh Basil Pesto

Although pesto is now frequently made from cilantro, parsley, spinach, mint, or a mixture of these greens, combined with walnuts or other nuts, here is the original version.

2 cups firmly packed fresh basil leaves, rinsed and dried
¼ cup pine nuts
3 garlic cloves, peeled
¾ cup freshly grated Parmesan cheese (about 3 ounces), preferably Parmigiano-Reggiano, or a blend of Parmesan and Romano cheeses
½ cup olive oil, preferably extra-virgin

Combine the basil, pine nuts, and garlic in a food processor or blender and purée. Blend in the cheese. With the motor running, slowly add the oil until well mixed.

Use immediately, or transfer to a container, cover with a thin layer of olive oil to keep the sauce from darkening, and refrigerate for up to 3 days.

Makes about 2 cups.

Butter, Cream, and Cheese Sauce (Alfredo)

This old standard originated in the Roman restaurant Alfredo's, where it has long been prepared with considerable flourish.

For a change of pace, substitute crumbled goat's milk cheese or creamy blue cheese for the usual Parmesan.

¾ cup (1½ sticks) unsalted butter
1½ cups heavy (whipping) cream
1½ cups freshly grated Parmesan cheese (about 6 ounces), preferably Parmigiano-Reggiano
Salt
Freshly ground black pepper
Freshly grated nutmeg

In a large, heavy saucepan, melt the butter over low heat; stir in the cream to heat through. Just before serving, add the cheese and stir until the cheese melts. Season to taste with salt, pepper, and nutmeg. Use immediately.

Makes about 2¾ cups.

Citrus Cream

This sauce is divine simplicity! It is especially good with freshly made noodles.

1 cup (2 sticks) unsalted butter
4 cups heavy (whipping) cream
½ cup freshly squeezed lemon, lime, or orange juice
Minced or grated zest of 8 to 10 lemons or limes, or 4 or 5 oranges
Salt
Freshly ground white pepper

Combine the butter and cream in a heavy saucepan. Bring to a boil, then stir in the juice and zest. Cook, stirring occasionally, until the mixture is reduced to 2 cups. Season to taste with salt and pepper. Use immediately, or set aside for up to 2 hours and slowly reheat just before serving.

Makes about 2 cups.

Herbed Cream

If the pasta is stuffed, choose an herb that is complementary to the ingredients.

2 tablespoons unsalted butter or olive oil
¼ cup chopped shallots or red onion
1 cup chopped fresh herbs such as basil or cilantro (coriander)
2 tablespoons dry white wine
3 cups heavy (whipping) cream
½ cup freshly grated Asiago or Parmesan cheese (about 2 ounces), preferably Parmigiano-Reggiano
Salt
Freshly ground white pepper

In a heavy saucepan over medium heat, melt the butter. Add the shallots or onion and sauté until soft, about 5 minutes. Add the herbs and wine and cook until the wine evaporates. Stir in the cream and cook, stirring frequently, until reduced by half. Add the cheese and season to taste with salt and pepper. When the cheese melts, transfer to a fine wire strainer or a chinois positioned over a clean saucepan and push the mixture through with a wooden spoon. Use immediately, or set aside for up to 2 hours and slowly reheat just before serving.

Makes about 1½ cups.

Saffron Sauce

I'm very fond of saffron, but you may prefer using less for a more delicate flavor.

3 tablespoons unsalted butter
½ cup minced shallot
½ cup dry white wine
½ cup homemade chicken stock or
    canned chicken broth
2½ teaspoons crumbled saffron
    threads
3 cups heavy (whipping) cream
Salt
Freshly ground white pepper

In a saucepan, melt the butter over medium-low heat. Add the shallot and cook, stirring frequently, until soft, about 10 minutes. Add the wine, stock or broth, and saffron and cook until the liquid evaporates. Stir in the cream and cook, stirring frequently, until reduced by half. Season to taste with salt and pepper. Use immediately, or set aside for up to 2 hours and slowly reheat just before serving.

Makes about 2 cups.

Eggplant Sauce

This is one of my very favorites when my tastebuds call for a simmered tomato-based sauce.

1 pound eggplant, cut into 1-inch
    cubes
2 tablespoons all-purpose flour
⅓ cup olive oil, preferably extra-
    virgin, or more if needed
½ cup chopped yellow onion
2 cups chopped peeled fresh or
    drained canned tomatoes
¾ cup tomato purée
¼ teaspoon sugar
Salt
Freshly ground black pepper
3 tablespoons chopped fresh basil

Sprinkle the eggplant with the flour and toss to coat well.

In a large, heavy saucepan, heat the oil over medium heat. Add the eggplant and sauté until lightly browned all over. Using a slotted utensil, transfer the eggplant to paper toweling to drain.

Add the onion to the saucepan, adding more oil, if necessary, and sauté until soft and lightly browned, about 7 minutes. Stir in the tomatoes, tomato purée, sugar, and salt and pepper to taste. Cook, stirring occasionally, for 20 minutes. Add the reserved eggplant and bring to a boil. Stir in the basil, reduce the heat to low, cover, and simmer until the eggplant is tender when pierced, about 20 minutes longer. Use immediately, or cover and refrigerate for up to 4 or 5 days. Reheat before serving.

Makes about 2 cups.

INDEX

RECIPE INDEX

INDEX TO PASTA RECIPES IN OTHER JAMES McNAIR COOKBOOKS

ACKNOWLEDGMENTS

All china has been provided by Taitu. Available in fine stores everywhere.

Neon sculptures on pages 24, 34, 37, 45, 54, 66, 72, 78, 83, and 84 are from The Right Light, San Francisco.

Neon tubes throughout the book are from Golden Gate Neon, San Francisco.

To everyone at Chronicle Books for a terrific job of editing, printing, distributing, and promoting my books.

To Cleve Gallat and David Kingins at CTA Graphics for their expertise in typesetting and mechanical production.

To Patricia Brabant and her assistant, M. J. Murphy, for another stunning success behind the camera and creating special effects with neon.

To my network of family and friends who encourage my efforts in myriad ways. Special thanks this time to Mark Leno for his advice on neon, and to Martha McNair and John Richardson for loaning cooking equipment for the studio.

To my assistant, Ellen Berger-Quan, for her invaluable contributions both in and out of the kitchen. I can't imagine how I ever worked without her.

To the rest of my crew Addie Prey, Buster Booroo, Joshua J. Chew, Michael T. Wigglebutt, and Dweasel Pickle for their tail-wagging compliments to the test kitchen results.

To my partner, Lin Cotton, for his stimulating ideas and keen sense of direction.